Child Abuse and Neglect:

A Teacher's Handbook for Detection, Reporting, and Classroom Management

The Consultants

Alfred Alschuler, Professor of Education, University of Massachusetts

Deborah Bacon, President, National Association of School Nurses, Inc./NEA

Annette Heiser Ficker, M.D., Children's Hospital National Medical Center

Isadora Hare, Senior Staff Associate, National Association of Social Workers

Hilda B. Minkoff, President, American School Counselor Association

Becky J. Smith, President, Association for the Advancement of Health Education-AAHPERD

The Review Board

For the names of the more than 500 educators who reviewed the manuscript in various stages, see pages 107-12.

Child Abuse and Neglect:

A Teacher's Handbook for Detection, Reporting, and Classroom Management

Cynthia Crosson Tower

nea PROFESSIONAL LIBRARY
National Education Association
Washington, D.C.

Acknowledgement

The NEA gratefully acknowledges the helpful information provided during the development of this book by the National Center on Child Abuse and Neglect, Washington, D.C.; the C. Henry Kempe National Center for the Prevention and Treatment of Child Abuse and Neglect, Denver, Colorado; and Herner and Company—Information Scientists, Arlington, Virginia.

Printing History:
   First Printing: March 1984
   Second Printing: July 1984
   Third Printing: February 1985

Library of Congress Cataloging in Publication Data

Tower, Cynthia Crosson.
   Child abuse and neglect.

   Includes bibliographies.
   1. Child abuse—United States. 2. Child abuse—Law
and legislation—United States. 3. Teacher-student
relationships. I. Title.
HV741.T68   1984   362.7'044   83-25071
ISBN 0-8106-0826-X (paper)
ISBN 0-8106-0827-8 (cloth)

Contents

The Author

Cynthia Crosson Tower is Associate Professor and Coordinator of the Human Services Program, Behavioral Science Department at Fitchburg State College, Massachusetts. She received her M.S.W. from the University of Connecticut and her B.A. from Western College for Women, Oxford, Ohio. Ms. Tower has been associated with the Massachusetts Department of Social Services in the Adoption Placement Unit, Protective Services, Family and Children's Services, and is a licensed clinical social worker. She has had extensive experience in writing and conducting training programs about child abuse and neglect, and is a frequent consultant on the subject for schools and social workers. She is also a fully certificated teacher of the Royal Scottish Country Dance Society, Edinburgh.

To

Chay, Jamie,

and

Fenneke

The NEA Policies on Child Abuse and Neglect

NEA RESOLUTION

B-35. Child Abuse

The National Education Association believes that all children should be protected from child abuse, including incest, and that educators are in a position to observe and recognize abuse which has been inflicted on children.

The Association and its affiliates should—

a. Cooperate with community organizations to increase public awareness and understanding of child abuse

b. Encourage the development and use of materials to increase student awareness of child abuse

c. Encourage development of teacher preparation courses and professional development programs that stress the identification of, reporting procedures for, and techniques in dealing with abused children

d. Encourage the development by affiliates of educator awareness programs dealing with the abused child.

The Association urges its affiliates to seek the enactment of state and local legislation that would—

a. Provide educators reporting suspected child abuse immunity from legal action

b. Require educators to report to the appropriate authorities instances of suspected child abuse

c. Provide for protection of children from other children. (74, 82)

NEA NEW BUSINESS ITEM

Child Abuse and Neglect

The National Education Association shall ally with other groups toward the objective of preventing child abuse and neglect. The NEA shall urge its state affiliates to pursue actively advocacy for the welfare of all children and shall advocate state funding and specific educational programs designed to prevent child abuse and neglect. (1982-61)

Foreword

AN EDUCATOR'S OVERVIEW OF CHILD ABUSE AND NEGLECT
by Alfred Alschuler, Ph.D., Professor of Education, University of Massachusetts

Some teachers are uncertain about the significance of the clues. Other teachers make accurate diagnoses but may not know what to do. Those who know, often are afraid to act. This book by Cynthia Tower will help overcome these problems. She demystifies the social, psychological, and legal aspects of child abuse and neglect. After reading this book, teachers will find the mechanics of detection and reporting to be very clear.

I would be proud to report that schools of education, or most schools of education, or even my own school of education, adequately prepare teachers to recognize these problems and to act effectively. I cannot make this claim. Schools of education are overburdened preparing teachers to instruct in the "basics," to solve other problems, or simply to survive teaching. But truly, is there anything more basic than helping to stop the destruction of children's bodies and the warping of their minds?

According to the psychoanalyst Erik Erickson, "the worst sin is the mutilation of a child's spirit." Abuse and neglect of children are heinous not only because youngsters are vulnerable and relatively powerless, but also because the effects of such maltreatment are so deep, so broad, and so long-lasting. As a clinical psychologist, I work with these victims of abuse and neglect as adults. Thirty years after being sexually abused as a four-year-old, one female client is still unable to relate meaningfully to men, has recurrent nightmares and heavy residues of anger and shame. Another client, who was physically abused as a child, married an abuser, but sought help only after his beatings extended beyond her to their children. This cycle may continue for generations. One neglected child years later completed her training as a nurse. Her professional competence is balanced by an equal and opposite homelife. Her nearly pathological tantrums, filthy home, jealousy, and infidelity are stunting her children's growth, destroying her marriage, and making her own consciousness hellish. Helping to stop child abuse and neglect simultaneously contains the long-term human costs, like spotting and stopping a contagious disease before it becomes an epidemic.

Ms. Tower's book authoritatively and realistically fills a gap in the information available to teachers. The rest is up to us. We need to use the information well, so that our students have a chance to become wholesome adults. Helping to stop child abuse and neglect is a courageous act of love.

THE SCHOOL NURSE'S ROLE, by Deborah Bacon, R.N. President, National Association of School Nurses, Inc./NEA

The National Committee for the Prevention of Child Abuse reported that one million children in the United States were physically, sexually, or emotionally abused or neglected during 1982. Because education is mandatory, a great number of these maltreated children attend school. The educational setting therefore affords the greatest opportunity for identification, intervention, and prevention of child abuse. A caring school staff can help improve the quality of life for these child victims.

School nurses are an integral part of the multidisciplinary approach to the care and treatment of maltreated children. Through the comprehensive school health records they keep on the student population, they can assist in identifying patterns indicative of child abuse. They can also help identify stressors within the child's family unit and make referrals to community agencies. Thus they can play a key role within the school setting to assist the classroom teacher in identifying, documenting, and reporting child abuse to the proper community agencies.

Because of their school-based practice, school nurses are in an excellent position to work with abused children. Although most of these professionals are not educationally prepared for intense counseling, they can offer the child an emotionally supportive relationship with a concerned adult. In addition, their expertise may enable them to facilitate the teacher-parent relationship. They can also be helpful in evaluating the intervention process at case conferences. And they should plan and assist in long-term followup for students and their families.

The classroom teacher can enlist the aid of the school nurse to help facilitate early detection of child abuse, to plan and/or provide refresher programs for school faculties, as well as to teach students to identify victims and seek help. The school nurse can also be the liaison between the school, the family, and the community agencies. Open communication is paramount for quality care of the abused child.

If your school district has no active child abuse team, enlist the school nurse to help initiate one. When in doubt about any aspect of reporting or care for one of your students, look to your school nurse as your ally.

THE PHYSICIAN'S ROLE, by Annette Heiser Ficker, M.D., Children's Hospital National Medical Center

Teachers, like physicians, are in a unique position to be advocates for children. By the very nature of their profession, they are advocates for all children. But to a special few (or many)—the children who are victims of violence or misuse in their own homes—teachers may be the only ally they have in the world. First of all, who else has access to these children outside of family members?...teachers when the children come to school or physicians when they come for health problems or checkups. These professionals are the ones who can be objective, who can recognize that a child is hurt, who can report to proper authorities and thus start the family on the way to repair.

In order to take these steps, there must be a willingness to accept the fact that children can be abused, to be aware of subtle signs and symptoms of abuse, and to have an available support system for making a decision to report, as well as a plan of continual encouragement to the child and the family.

There are many professionals who want to avoid this issue because it is too painful or they do not believe it. An advocate is one who will take risks for another when no one else will. There is not much risk in these instances since in most states only suspicion of abuse must be reported and there is immunity for those who report in good faith. It is also helpful to realize that many parents who abuse their children really do not want to do so and wish they could stop. But as with many social problems or addictions, they cannot help themselves—they cannot cure themselves. In many ways these parents seem to be begging to be identified. Physicians see this in the emergency room or clinic when parents bring in a child with apparent injuries which in no way could have been caused by the history they give. We could have helped them make up a better story. Or they keep returning to the same hospital week after week waiting for someone to see that these "accidents" are too numerous to occur over such a short period of time. Why do they keep returning? Why do they keep sending the child to school with sometimes obvious injuries? They are crying for help. More likely they were abused as children themselves and grew up not feeling good about themselves. Even though they may show a defensive and angry attitude, underneath they are most insecure and helpless.

The more support the teacher has in the school and community, the easier it is to make a necessary report. It is always a good idea to talk over one's suspicion of abuse with another peer, or better still with the principal, counselor, or school nurse. There should also be the opportunity to discuss such problems in a multidisciplinary forum. Yet the decision to report ultimately rests with the one who suspects.

It is good for teachers to have in place community experts whom they can consult also. A good way to build these relationships is to have protective service workers, youth division officers of the police department, and/or pediatricians come and speak at in-service training sessions. These experts can provide valuable support, initially in making a report, later in helping to manage the child and the family through the crisis, and even later through the healing stage.

What a great opportunity teachers have to administer to children and families in so many ways; at the same time, what a grave responsibility they have to advocate.

THE SOCIAL WORKER'S ROLE, by Isadora Hare, M.S.W., Senior Staff Associate, National Association of Social Workers

The origin of the movement to protect children from abuse and neglect is often attributed to the case of Mary Ellen in New York City in 1875 when the Society for the Prevention of Cruelty to Animals used animal protection laws to remove a child from her abusive foster parents. This case led to the formation of Societies for the Prevention of Cruelty to Children. Since that time social workers in public and private agencies have been in the forefront of services to provide protection to abused and neglected children. In the 1950's and early 1960's, advances in medical science led to improved detection of child maltreatment and stirred public interest to the point that child abuse reporting laws were passed and a multidisciplinary approach to the problem was developed.

The role of teachers in this interprofessional effort is crucial. No other profession is better placed to observe a wider group of school-age children, and to the child, the teacher is the most accessible adult outside the family to provide help in time of trouble. Furthermore, schools are part of the everyday lives of people in the community, and families with problems can relate easily to them.

As a social worker turned educator, Cynthia Tower constantly stresses the importance of collaboration between teachers and social workers in their mutual goal of promoting the child's healthy development. Teachers are vital links in community efforts to identify, treat, and prevent child maltreatment. However, the current demands on teachers to perform a variety of functions are enormous. In 1983, numerous national reports emphasized that if we are to improve the standard of education—if we are to combat mediocrity and seek excellence—teachers need more time to concentrate on teaching and to be freed from other obligations and interruptions.

The school social worker can play a major role in ensuring teacher participation in cases of abuse, while relieving educators of some of the attendant time-consuming burdens. Social workers in schools are both educational personnel and social workers. Because of their knowledge of the educational system and of social welfare agencies, they can be helpful as a contact between the school and protective service agencies. As part of their job they make home visits, and their training in dealing with difficult family situations enables them to aid teachers in assessing whether a child is abused or neglected to the point that a report is required. In addition to being available to act as consultants to teachers and principals on the various difficult aspects of the problem and the phases of intervention, they can provide in-service training and courses to teachers on the topic. Equally important, either alone, or in cooperation with the protective services social worker, school social workers can act as broker, putting troubled families in touch with community resources. Furthermore, their participation in committee meetings reviewing children's special needs, and their assessment of the child's socioeconomic background can be helpful in determining whether a child needs special education, a child abuse or neglect report, or other special services in the school. And they are available to represent the school on the community's multidisciplinary team and to talk to PTAs and other groups about the school's role in treatment and prevention programs.

In many school districts one school social worker serves several schools. Consequently, this professional's time is limited. However, some areas have introduced innovative schemes in which certain school social workers are assigned as special consultants in abuse and neglect, available on call. In this way, school social workers can be additionally helpful to teachers as they perform their vital task in protecting children from maltreatment.

THE SCHOOL COUNSELOR'S ROLE, by Hilda B. Minkoff, Ed.D., President, American School Counselor Association

The incidence of child abuse and neglect and its reporting are among the chief concerns of our nation's counselors. In 1981, the American School Counselor Association (ASCA) adopted a position statement on child abuse and neglect because of the significant increase of incidences and the fact that school counselors are either legally mandated reporters or otherwise involved with such cases. The ASCA position statement provides policy, referral procedures, and other information needed by counselors. (Copies are available from ASCA, 5999 Stevenson Avenue, Alexandria, Virginia 22304.)

ASCA recognizes that the reporting of suspected cases of child abuse to the proper authorities is the responsibility of school counselors. Counselors, however, are not required to prove abuse or determine the child's need for protection. They are encouraged to report suspected cases to the principal or the administrative designee, who will then review the report and the school information with appropriate staff members including the teacher, the nurse, and the counselor. In many schools, counselors serve as designees due to their pivotal role as liaison between school, home, and community.

In many schools, the counselor is the only "constant" in a student's life. Generally, even in elementary schools, one teacher is no longer the sole educator of each child. From the middle school years upward, many students are taught by several different teachers.

By role and function, counselors are in a position to have close working relationships with community agencies and families. Within the school, counselors cannot and should not function in isolation. Teacher/counselor cooperation is a must in the delivery of all student services, and crucial in child abuse cases. A healthy and close working relationship between teachers and counselors can facilitate the detection and reporting of cases of abuse or neglect; it can also expedite the process of treatment for family members in need of help. A feeling of respect between these two professionals permits teachers to draw upon counselor expertise in the student developmental process and during the crises and environmental stresses that affect family life. Cooperative involvement of both professionals in in-service education programs for detecting abuse and neglect and for becoming familiar with state reporting requirements can also raise the level of mutual respect and point out counselor strengths in school/community agency interaction.

Another mutual activity, the offering of parenting courses, can help all parents feel closer to the school. In these various ways, teachers and counselors working together can make a very strong weapon to decrease the incidence of child abuse and neglect.

THE HEALTH EDUCATOR'S ROLE, by Becky J. Smith, Ph.D., President, Association for the Advancement of Health Education-AAHPERD (1982-84)

Child abuse and neglect is of critical concern to health educators at all levels. The primary objective of health education is the promotion of health and well-being. In confronting and reporting cases of child abuse and neglect, health educators are faced with a dynamic problem that may affect the well-being not only of the current generation but also of future generations of children. In addition, the health education curriculum can provide an equally important interaction with this subject area.

Health is quality in life; the potential for health is in direct ratio to the development of individual human potential. Much of this development is influenced by experiencing positive interactions during childhood. When these interactions become negative, they hamper the processes of growth and development and may result in distress and illness.

Educators, particularly health educators, can help all children by creating and maintaining a healthful school environment. Such an environment can provide both young children and adolescents with an image of healthy human functioning in the presence of a mature, loving person.

It is also important that all children begin to study and understand abusive behavior and neglect as early as possible. At the same time, however, it is important that they study the positive concepts of love, nurturing, and healthy emotional expression. Health education classes need to provide a forum for positive alternatives to the abuse and neglect that some students may be experiencing as well as studying.

The family, the school, and society all share a responsibility for creating and maintaining an atmosphere that facilitates health and well-being. Health educators can contribute to this process by helping to develop health education and parent education programs that include a broad-based examination of forces and factors in child abuse and neglect. Health education curricula in secondary schools need to go beyond the formal study of child abuse and neglect to encompass the study of social services and parenting skills. Such programs will better prepare students to recognize, report, and follow through any cases of abuse or neglect they may encounter. They will also more fully prepare graduates to undertake the role and responsibility of parenthood and to work with educators, health professionals, social service workers, and all others striving to prevent child abuse and neglect.

Preface

Why should the classroom teacher or any school official be concerned about child abuse or neglect? Isn't this the arena of the social worker? Educators have a duty to become involved in detecting and reporting abuse and neglect for at least three reasons. First, the trauma created by abuse and neglect is as much a detriment to learning as a perceptual or physical difficulty. Every year millions of dollars are spent to ensure that the perceptually impaired child is able to learn. Yet unless the abused child also happens to have a categorized perceptual problem, that child may go unaided.

Studies of learning patterns show that in order to learn, students must be sufficiently free from discomfort and conflict to channel their energies into comprehension. Yet the abused or neglected child may be expending this valuable energy on merely coping with the home situation. Only through treatment—the relief of this pressure—can the child be freed to take full advantage of the learning opportunities available. By detecting the abuse or neglect and facilitating such treatment, the teacher enhances the child's ability to learn.

The second reason why educators should become involved in the detection and reporting of child abuse and neglect is that their role places them in close contact with the child on a daily basis. Classroom teachers, especially, see the child in a variety of situations and may be privy to some of the most intimate information of the child's life. Not only do teachers have more contact than any other adult, except the caretaker, but they also have a tremendous amount of influence on the developing youngster. They are in an excellent position to help the child deal with concerns that are barriers to learning.

The third and most undeniable reason for educators' being concerned about child abuse and neglect is that in all states teachers are mandated to report child abuse and can in fact be held liable for failure to do so.

Why are teachers not involved more often? It has been my observation that they may not be more involved for several reasons: (1) they may not know exactly how to recognize abuse or neglect; (2) they may not feel comfortable reporting the abuse or neglect due to their own disbelief, a need to deny this frightening phenomenon, or the perceived or actual lack of support by administrators; or (3) once they accept the reality of abuse or neglect, they do not know exactly how or where to report it or what the legal implications are for themselves.

This handbook is dedicated to teachers, in recognition of their attempts to provide the best possible education for children. I have tried to answer the questions that teachers most often ask about recognizing abuse, neglect, and sexual abuse, and the necessity and logistics of reporting.

In many instances, the nature of the material requires the use of clinical, biological terms. It is essential to be specific so that all who are concerned about these issues can understand exactly what is involved. It is also important to speak clearly and realistically about the nature of these problems, avoiding euphemisms or evasions, in order to deal with them and work toward prevention.

In addition, I have attempted to give a picture not only of the abusive or neglectful parent, but also of the social service system that acts upon the report made by the educator. As a social worker turned educator, it is my feeling that the teacher and the social worker are invaluable to each other in their mutual goal—enhancing the child's chances for a healthy development. During my years as a protective social worker, I realized the importance of the teacher's role in maltreatment situations—from initial detection to further validation to later assistance in treatment efforts through classroom activities to prevention. Now, as a teacher, I continue to work with social workers to strengthen the bond of these two professions. This handbook is another attempt to do so.

I would like to recognize the assistance and support of the many who made this book possible. The members of the Review Board who took time to write letters and suggest revisions based upon their own experiences and frustrations have made this undertaking more comprehensive. My consultations with Alexis Eaton, Kent Dumas, Liz Nyman, Linda Gates, Kay Simms, Carolyn Olson, and my good friend and colleague, Susan McCauley, have aided my understanding and enabled me to present a more complete picture. I thank Nancy Moses for her time and energy, and I am especially indebted to Muriel Crosson for her encouragement as well as for her excellent editing and typing. My husband, Charles, and my children have been patient and have given me a great deal of support in this venture, for which I am very grateful. I would also like to thank those mentors who have encouraged and believed in me, Carel Germaine and Al Alschuler. Finally, I do not believe any such work would have been possible had it not been for my teacher in writing and in life, James Cope Crosson.

—Cynthia Crosson Tower

Chapter 1

How Do You Recognize Abuse and Neglect?

A breathless, harried high school teacher greeted me as I arrived to conduct in-service training on abuse and neglect for a group of local teachers.

"I'm so glad you're here!" he breathed, and then proceeded to recount his day's activity attempting to report a suspected case of abuse of a 14-year-old student.

"I shouldn't have waited so long, but I just wasn't sure and didn't know whom to tell!" He had finally told the school nurse, and for the rest of the day, he and she had tried to contact the appropriate agency. Feeling that it was his duty to do so, he had also told the mother of his intent. The mother, fearful of her abusive husband, had picked up the child and fled. Now after hours, the confused teacher was left not knowing whom to go to, not knowing if the child was in danger, and agonizing over his role in the entire matter.

It became painfully obvious to me as I tried to help this teacher—to identify the proper agency to which to make the report and to elicit a promise from social services that the case would be treated as an emergency—that he might well exemplify the plight of many teachers when they are faced with one of society's most difficult problems. I considered how many other educators would benefit from the knowledge of exactly what to do in such a crisis situation.

Concerned teachers are not only confronted with possible physical abuse of children;* they may also encounter physical neglect, sexual abuse, and emotional abuse as well. This chapter examines each of these types of abuse.

PHYSICAL ABUSE

Physical abuse refers to a nonaccidental physical injury to a child. The most obvious way to detect it is by outward physical signs such as the following:

- extensive bruises, especially numerous bruises of different colors,

---

*Child or children as used in this book (unless otherwise defined) refers to any person under 18 years of age.

indicating various stages of healing (strange bruises are always possible in normal activities; it is their frequency that arouses suspicions of abuse)

Ages of bruises can be approximately detected by the following colors:

Immediate-few hours = red
6-12 hours = blue
12-24 hours = black-purple
4-6 days = green tint, dark
5-10 days = pale green to yellow (9, p.8)*

- burns of all types (although burns may also be accidental), but especially glove-like burns, which indicate that the hand has been immersed in hot liquid; burns that are more intense in the middle and radiate from there, which could indicate that hot liquid has been poured onto the skin; cigarette burns; burns in the shape of an object such as a poker, an iron
- bruises in specific shapes such as handprints, hanger marks
- frequent complaints of soreness or awkward movements, as if caused by pain
- marks that indicate hard blows from an object such as an electrical cord or other whiplike object that could make a burn around the body
- bruises on multiple parts of the body indicating blows from different directions
- unexplained abdominal swelling (may be caused by internal bleeding)
- extreme sensitivity to pain
- frequent bruises around the head or face (the area of other bruises may be important—knees and elbows, for example, are especially vulnerable in normal falls; bruises to the abdomen or midway between the wrist and elbow may be more unlikely in normal activities)
- bald spots indicative of severe hair pulling.

The key thing to look for in physical abuse is an explanation that does not fit the injury. For example, the child reports a "fall" while the bruises indicate the clear outline of an object such as a belt, or the child who "fell off the bed" is too severely bruised for such a fall.

Behaviorally, children also give many clues.

---

*Numbers in parentheses appearing in the text refer to the Bibliography beginning on page 79.

Kara, age 5, always presented a neat, well-ordered picture. Although not expensive, her clothes were well-chosen, clean, and pressed. Her long-sleeved blouses and colorful tights seemed a bit strange in warmer weather, but the teacher made no comments about them. The child was very affectionate, almost to the point of smothering; her endearing ways made her an easy candidate for teacher's pet. It was not until Kara unexplainably wet her pants and the teacher helped her remove her tights to clean up, that anything seemed amiss. Kara's small legs revealed numerous bruises in various stages of healing. An examination by the school nurse attested to the abuse Kara had suffered over her entire body.

Joe was not a difficult child, nor was he unlikable. He was just "there" in the classroom of 30 other bubbling, boisterous youngsters. He did his work as instructed and never talked back. His only problem was frequently falling asleep. Joe's "accidents"— the bruises in September, the broken arm in January, and the burned hands in March—did not even raise the teacher's suspicions. When the teacher made a special effort to talk with apparently shy Joe, the story came out. He had been abused by his mother for several years.

Kevin, a boisterous, unruly, and pugnacious child, spent a good deal of time sitting in the assistant principal's office. Most of the teachers at the junior high school dreaded his appearance in class. In the past year he had run away from home. In fact, his biggest fear was that the school would call his home. It was not until the school received word from the local social service agency that Kevin had been removed from his home due to life-threatening abuse, that the cause of his behavior became more apparent.

The three preceding vignettes depict examples of reactions that children may exhibit to abuse. Kara's story speaks of a well-ordered home where expectations run high. Her desire to please within this rigid framework transfers itself to school as well. Joe's behavior is probably indicative of the most prolonged, severe abuse. Here is a child who has turned inward, who may spend his nighttime hours wakeful, fearing more abuse, and his daytime hours fighting his body's need for sleep. He describes himself as accident-prone, protecting the homelife he is convinced he deserves.

While the problems of Kara and Joe may go unnoticed by some, Kevin's problem is more obvious. Kevin is striking out at the world, which appears to give him nothing but abuse. He is at the hub of an ever-moving wheel of abuse and misperception. At home he is beaten by an alcoholic father who spends his sober hours expounding the virtues of machismo. His attempts to cry for help in school translate into disruptive behavior and meet with more rejection. If his parents are called in, the cycle repeats itself.

Behaviorally, there are a number of ways to recognize the abused child. Kara, Joe, and Kevin exemplify several characteristics:

- overcompliance
- withdrawal, perpetual sleepiness
- acting out, aggressive, disruptive behavior.

Other behavioral symptoms to consider are the following:

- destructiveness to self and others
- coming to school too early or leaving late—a clear indicator of fear of going home
- cheating, stealing, or lying (this may be related to too high expectations at home)
- accident proneness (ruling out organic problems, such behavior may be unconsciously self-destructive; if the accidents are "reported" but do not happen at school, it may be a coverup for abuse)
- fearfulness (the child may assume that adults hurt and is constantly on guard)
- low achievement (in order to learn, children must convert aggressive energy into learning; children who are either overly aggressive or lacking in energy may have little or no energy for learning)
- inability to form good peer relationships (many abusive parents prohibit their child from seeking out friends, perhaps because of fear of exposure)
- wearing clothing that covers the body and that may be inappropriate for warm months
- dislike of or shrinking from physical contact (the child may not tolerate physical praise such as a pat on the back)
- regressiveness, exhibiting less mature behavior. (See Appendix A for a quick reference chart of physical and behavioral indicators.)

These symptoms apply to adolescents as well as to younger children. The abuse of adolescents is also a major problem, although many do not recognize it as such for several reasons:

1. Adolescents do not fit the picture of child victims.
2. Adolescents may have as much strength or weight as adults.
3. Adolescents may be provocative (physically, verbally, or sexually).

4. Adolescents seem capable of better impulse control than younger children.
5. Adolescents may be perceived as able to run away from or avoid an abusive situation.
6. Adolescents may appear to have access to more potential help (such as police or social services) outside the family. (14, p.18)

Despite the apparent advantages of adolescents over younger children, in an abusive situation, they are still hampered by ties and remnants of family dependence from childhood. Adolescents need to be seen as independent, but their history has probably been one of returning to the family for safety. They may also have come to believe that any fault lies with them rather than with the family.

In addition to the symptoms noted, which are obvious in younger children, certain behavioral indicators, although perhaps true of younger children, are seen especially in adolescents. Abuse is suspect in adolescents who—

- overreact to being touched in any way (react with fear or aggression).
- seem to provoke encounters of abusive treatment from adults as well as from peers.
- demonstrate extremes in behavior—either great hostility and aggressiveness or withdrawal.
- exhibit assaultive, aggressive, or pugnacious behavior.
- appear to be overly frightened of parents.
- act out continually or are described as incorrigible. (14, p.13)

When considering adolescent abuse, the school is decidedly the *most* important link in the helping chain. The teacher is the professional *most* likely to detect abuse in this age group and is in the best position to report. Younger children may come to the attention of members of the medical profession; as a rule, abused teens do not.

Keep in mind, however, that observing one or two of these symptoms in any age group does not *necessarily* mean abuse. It does mean that you should be watchful—carefully observing the child for additional indicators. Many of the factors mentioned may be indicative of other problems as well. In addition, there are cultural factors to consider. For example, some Vietnamese children may suffer from unusual bruises around the head and neck resulting from common folk remedies for headaches or colds. Long-sleeved shirts or pants worn by Moslem girls may be a custom rather than a response to the weather or a coverup for abuse. Documenting strange or unusual behavior can help the unsure teacher accumulate a variety of clues and perhaps become aware of an abusive pattern.

Remember that emotionally, physical abuse affects children in many ways. Victims suffer from poor self-image, feelings of little self-worth and, perhaps, that they deserve the abuse. In addition, they may have learned that adults will hurt them; therefore they are watchful and untrusting. Children reflect their family life. Those who present a negative, depressed picture may well be mirroring the unrest at home—if not actual abuse, certainly some other kind of family disturbance.

PHYSICAL NEGLECT

Physical neglect refers to the failure on the part of the caretaker to meet the child's basic physical needs.

My first impresssion of Robbie was of the dull appearance of his hair and eyes. Somehow this was even more striking than the odor emanating from his corner desk. Sullen and quiet, Robbie drifted through my first grade lessons, barely able to find a pencil in his disorganized desk. His lunch usually consisted of Twinkies, which he said he bought on his walk to school. Later I learned that he more frequently stole them from the corner store. He eyed the other children's lunches covetously, and once I saw him steal an apple when a classmate turned her back. Quickly, like a furtive animal, he thrust the apple into the pocket of his dirty, faded, tattered pants.

Notes and phone calls to his parents met with no response. Robbie was a sad little nomad, drifting into school and listlessly returning home, reportedly to take care of his younger brother and sister.

Robbie is not unlike many other neglected children. Teachers ofter remark upon their general dull appearance. In addition, these victims of neglect—

- may appear in soiled clothing, significantly too small or too large and often in need of repair.
- always seem to be hungry, hoarding or stealing food but coming to school with little of their own.
- may appear listless and tired.
- often report caring for younger siblings, when the child caretaker may be only 5, 6, 7, or 8.
- demonstrate poor hygiene, may smell of urine, or have bad breath or obviously dirty teeth (although inconsistent bathing may be in vogue for teenagers, this practice should be distinguishable from the condition of the chronically unbathed, unkempt child).
- have unattended medical or dental problems such as infected sores or badly decayed or abscessed teeth.

- may have lice.
- may exhibit stealing, vandalism, or other delinquent behavior.
- may have frequent school absences or tardiness.
- have poor peer relationships, perhaps because of hygienic problems or a depressed, negative attitude.
- may be withdrawn.
- may crave affection, even eliciting negative responses to accomplish it.
- may be destructive or pugnacious, showing no apparent guilt over their acts.
- may be inadequately dressed for the weather.
- may be emaciated or may have distended stomachs indicative of malnutrition. (See Appendix A for a quick reference chart of these indicators.)

Neglected adolescents tend to demonstrate many of these symptoms, but they may escape the well-intended intervention of educators by dropping out of school. They may also exhibit a pattern of early emancipation from their families with the promise of drifting into unfulfilled or even crime-ridden lives.

Neglected children of all ages are accustomed to a lifestyle devoid of routine and organization. They may demonstrate this in their own lives. For example, an inability to organize, or a lack of cleanliness and order is not unlikely. It is important to realize that many neglected children represent just one more generation characterized by their lifestyle. Their grandparents' teachers may also have been concerned with similar problems. Children learn parenting from their parents—they are their role models. Generation after generation of inadequate and neglectful role models, with no intervention, will create individuals who are only negatively prepared for parenting. Because of its pervasive nature, neglect is difficult to deal with. Where does the cycle end in the cases of parents with unmet needs who, in turn, are unable to meet the needs of their offspring? Only through intervention can this neglectful pattern be changed. Although children may be adequately fed and clothed, taught proper hygiene and given affection and attention, their parents too must be helped in order to break the cycle of neglect. This topic is discussed in Chapter 8.

SEXUAL ABUSE

Debbie, 14, had a "reputation" in school. She was not popular in the healthy sense of the word, she was talked about. Teachers observed her provocative behavior in their classes. According to rumors she could be approached by any boy who sought a sexual experience. The tight-fitting clothes over her well-developed figure necessitated several visits to the assistant principal who tried to encourage more appropriate dress. School personnel assumed that her behavior was indicative of an inappropriately expressed sexual awakening colored by a poor self-image. When Debbie finally ran away from home, the story came out. She had been sexually abused by her father since the age of 9.

Sexual abuse has always been a human problem, but there has perhaps never been more awareness of it than at present. Social workers estimate that between 60 and 75 percent of the reported cases of child abuse are of sexual abuse. There is no way of knowing how many cases go unreported due to the taboo nature of this topic. It is safe to assume, however, that the problem is a major one. As in Debbie's case, the symptoms may be mistaken for other problems.

What is meant by sexual abuse? It refers to sexual involvement imposed upon a child by an adult who has greater "power, knowledge, and resources" (35, p.78). David Finkelhor points out the child's inability to consent, which, he says, is based upon knowledge and authority, neither of which is at the child's command (12).

Throughout her whole first grade year, six-year-old June had had at least six urinary tract infections, for which she was medicated periodically. Her teacher wondered if there were any tie between this problem and sexual abuse. The teacher knew that June's mother worked nights and that her new husband of 18 months babysat for June and her three-year-old brother.

It should be mentioned that aside from irritations from some forms of bubble bath and other rare, organic causes, it is not common for little girls to have the frequent urinary tract infections with which adult women may be plagued. The appearance of such recurrent infections would (at least) suggest the possibility of sexual abuse as the cause. As the story unfolded, it became evident that June was being sexually abused by her stepfather. Her teacher's report made it possible for the family to receive much needed help.

The most classic myth regarding sexual abuse is that it is perpetrated by strangers. Parents tell their children not to talk to strangers and not to take candy from strangers, for example. Certainly this is good parental advice. The fact remains, however, that between 70 and 85 percent of sexual abuse is committed by someone known—and often loved—by the child. Most perpetrators are male, although females are sometimes reported. The victims may be female or male, but females are more frequently seen in reports.

Children may be sexually abused at any age, but those who are prepubescent may be at more risk, due to their budding sexuality. By the time the abuse is uncovered, in most cases it has been continuing for between one and three years. According to Suzanne Sgroi, sexual abuse is characterized by a progression of sexual activity (37). It may begin with disrobing on the part of the perpetrator, or close observation of the child during bathing, dressing, or elimination rituals. Many sexual encounters begin with apparently innocent "horseplay" or kissing and progress to fondling, genital exposure, and mutual masturbation. Oral-genital contact, as well as anal contact, may follow, depending upon the opportunities available and the willingness of the child. Vaginal penetration with the fingers or penis often happens only after the perpetrator has carefully moved the child along to a level of readiness and trust. Experts are discovering, however, that even the first phases can create guilt and shame and can be almost as damaging as later phases (37, pp. 10-11).

Secrecy is a very important part of the whole picture in sexual abuse. While physical abuse may have its element of secrecy, society's horror of sexual deviation creates a need in the perpetrator to be especially careful in compelling quiet in the victim. Although threats or special attention may be enough to ensure some children's silence, sexual abusers may also use gifts, money, special outings, or edible treats. Charlotte Vale Allen in her account of her own sexual abuse speaks of finding change in her pockets after her father's abuse (1). Elements of this secrecy may be exhibited in a variety of ways. For example, the child may refuse to undress for gym, feeling that the teacher or peers can detect the sexual abuse just by seeing the unclothed body. It should be noted that failure to report sexual abuse can actually perpetuate the secrecy by aiding the perpetrator rather than the child.

Indicators of sexual abuse include the following:

- frequent urinary infections
- an inordinate number of gifts, or money from a questionable source
- exceptional secrecy
- more sexual knowledge than is appropriate for the child's age (especially in younger children)
- in-depth sexual play with peers (in younger children different from the normal "playing doctor" form of exploration)
- overcompliance or withdrawal
- overaggressiveness, acting out
- sexually provocative or promiscuous behavior (in adolescents) or otherwise acting out sexually
- an inordinate fear of males or seductiveness toward males
- a drop in school performance or sudden nonparticipation in school activities

27

- sleep problems such as nightmares or insomnia
- crying without provocation
- rashes or itching in genital areas, scratching the area a great deal or fidgeting when seated
- sudden onset of enuresis (wetting pants or bed) or soiling
- sudden phobic behavior
- symptoms associated with venereal disease, such as—vaginal pain, vaginal or penile discharge (in young children), genital or oral sores, frequent sore throats (may indicate gonococcal infection of the pharynx or throat)
- diagnosis of genital warts
- feelings of little self-worth, talk of being "damaged"
- pain in the genital area (which may be from lacerations)
- excessive bathing
- frequent vomiting
- excessive masturbation
- appearing much older and more worldly than peers
- great anxiety
- suicide attempts (especially among adolescents)
- runaway from home, excessively (epecially adolescents)
- early pregnancies (in adolescents). (See Appendix A for a quick reference chart of these indicators.)

It is easier to deny the symptoms of sexual abuse than it is to overlook physical abuse or neglect. It is also not quite so difficult to imagine that a prominent member of the community has "disciplined a child a little too severely"—perhaps because of stress—as it is to entertain the idea that he has been sexually involved with his daughter.

For sexual abuse to occur, several contributing factors are necesssary. The first is *opportunity*. Often there is the profile of a mother who works in the evening or at other times when a child may be most vulnerable. Or a mother may not be otherwise available—during times of illness, depression, or involvement outside the home, for example. Many sources also caution against the teenage male babysitter who is not involved with his peers and who does not have a strong male figure with whom to identify.

Another contributing factor to sexual abuse is *change*. Families have frequently undergone some recent stress such as relocation, unemployment, newly employed mother, or illness, which makes the members vulnerable. Many families may be candidates for either sexual or physical abuse due to frequent moves. Also present in many sexual abuse situations is the phenomenon of trust. More often than not, perpetrators occupy or assume a position that the child trusts, which makes their actions possible.

Some attention should be given to "stranger danger," the assault (usually one-time) of a child by a stranger. Although the family may not appear to be directly involved in such cases, it is vital that family members, too, receive help and possibly treatment. The trauma of child molestation is devastating to some families; the parents' reaction may well determine the child's ability to handle the memory in later life (37, p. 111).

Although teachers will be most aware of the child's involvement, it is well to keep in mind that physical and sexual abuse, as well as neglect, are family problems; in order that the child may be best helped, family involvement is important. Some family situations exhibit symptoms of both abuse and neglect. The prognosis for such cases is much poorer as the problems are compounded. Early reporting is therefore vital.

EMOTIONAL ABUSE

Emotional abuse refers to belittling, rejecting, and in general not providing a positive, loving, emotional atmosphere in which a child can grow.

This is perhaps the most difficult area to detect or prove and certainly difficult to report. Social service agencies are so overwhelmed with physical and sexual injuries that the less concrete report of emotional abuse may be screened out. That is, an agency may decide after reviewing the evidence that it is insufficient to warrant further investigation. This type of abuse is no less frustrating for the classroom teacher, however.

Tom, psychologically abused by his father, did not have the emotional strength necessary to learn to read in the first, second, or third grades. He just sat in school and relaxed in the warm, loving atmosphere. Outwardly cheerful and happy, his way of coping was to turn all negative incidents into jokes, but he manifested his problems by bizarre behavior such as eating (and swallowing) his shirts.

Indicators of emotional abuse, some of which Tom demonstrated, include the following:
- inappropriate affect such as turning negatives into jokes, or laughing when in pain
- extremes in behavior—overly happy or affectionate
- withdrawal—or no verbal or physical communication with others
- bizarre behavior such as self-destruction
- destructive behavior
- inordinate attention to details
- cruelty, vandalism, stealing, cheating
- rocking, thumbsucking, enuresis, or other habitual problems

- substance abuse (drugs or alcohol)
- anorexia nervosa (especially in adolescents)
- physical manifestations such as asthma, ulcers, or severe allergies
- delinquent behavior (especially in adolescents). (See Appendix A for a quick reference chart of these indicators)

Emotionally abusive parents may have unrealistically high expectations of their offspring. When the children are unable to meet these expectations they receive verbal criticism that makes them feel incompetent and generally "bad." Such expectations may be related to some values or ideas the parent holds, as the following example illustrates:

Sally demonstrated her abuse by a perpetually sad expression. She looked as if she had just been beaten, but her father never touched her. Instead he berated her: "How did I ever deserve a girl? Girls are lesser beings." He had her hair cut in an unbecoming style, saying there was no point in trying to make an ugly girl look any better. He demanded complete obedience and subservience, including having her stand beside him as he ate to cut and salt his food. He rationalized this activity saying that her only hope in life was to be of use to a husband, if in fact anyone would want her. Even when Sally scored 160·on an IQ test, her father assured her the teachers were wrong—she was only a girl. Unfortunately she believed him.

Children suffering from emotional abuse may exhibit much the same behavior (in terms of acting out or exhibiting a poor self-image) as those suffering from physical abuse. In some cases, the emotionally neglected child may be generally ignored. In the J. family, for example, 16-year-old Tammie did not meet the family's standards of high intelligence. She was treated as if she did not exist, while her sisters and brothers received parental attention and concern.

Unfortunately emotional abuse may not be easy to pinpoint. Many situations are not as clear-cut as those suggested here. Although most state statutes mention emotional abuse, it is difficult to prove. Teachers can help these child victims, however, with attention and encouragement to express themselves. (See Chapter 6 for specific suggestions.) In some cases the parents may merely need to know more about their child's need or they may need counseling to help them with their own problems.

Chapter 2

Whom Do You Tell?— The Reporting Process

The previous chapter discussed many of the clues to look for in detecting child abuse. Once teachers are satisfied that they have indeed recognized such clues, it is necessary that they report suspected cases of abuse. First, however, there are three kinds of knowledge with which well-prepared educators should be armed even *before* encountering a case of child maltreatment. They are as follows:

1. Knowledge of the reporting laws of the state in which they teach
2. Knowledge of the school reporting policy or procedure, if one is available—for example, an outline of the steps to follow within the school or information on when a report should be made
3. Knowledge of or a relationship with (either through the school or personally) the protective agency designated to accept reports.

This chapter discusses these three kinds of knowledge.

STATE REPORTING LAWS

What is the legal role of the teacher in reporting the abuse and neglect of children? All states expect educators to be involved in reporting; many states back up this expectation with a fine (which in some cases may be up to $1,000) or a jail sentence for failure to report. The teacher is frequently referred to as a *mandated reporter*—that is, one who in his or her professional capacity is legally responsible for reporting to the local protective agency. In addition to educators, state statutes designate other mandatory reporters, including other school personnel, and the extent of their responsibility. (See Appendix B for a list of reporters.) Every school system, if not every teacher, should have a copy of the state regulations concerning reporting. They can usually be obtained through the local protective agency. Many agencies also publish interpretations of the statutes that are much easier to read and understand than the laws themselves. Appendix D contains a list of regional resource centers, which not only publish newsletters in the field but also may be able to provide copies of state reporting laws and other information.

Liability is another issue that concerns educators. As mentioned earlier, there may be a fine or a jail sentence for *not* reporting. All states provide immunity for any professional who reports. (See Appendix E.) Various states protect the mandated reporter who reports "in good faith" or who has "reasonable cause to suspect abuse" (5, pp. 4-7). It is highly unlikely that an educator would be sued for reporting. Even if this did happen, the teacher who reported in good faith would not be found liable.

Whatever your state's stand on immunity, it is better legally and morally to report than not to report. Certainly it is wiser to make the local agency aware of a situation than to wait and perhaps subject a child to the risk of permanent harm or possible death.

SCHOOL REPORTING POLICY

Although anyone associated with the school system is responsible for reporting, it is important that the system have, or at least begin to set up, a procedure for reporting. Such a policy should include specific information such as the following:

1. At what point should the teacher report child abuse? Suspicion? Reasonable cause to believe? (This may be based not only on school policy but also on state law.)
2. Whom does the teacher notify? Nurse? Principal? School social worker?
3. What specific information does the teacher need to know to report?
4. What actions should the teacher have taken before reporting to validate suspicions?
5. What other school personnel should be involved?
6. Who makes the report to the appropriate authorities? How?
7. What information should be included in the report? (This may be dictated by state law and protective agency policy.)
8. What followup is expected on reported cases?
9. What role will the school play in possible community/child protection teams?
10. What commitment does the school have to in-service training or community programs?

The existence of such a policy and knowledge of it in advance will be extremely helpful to teachers. Immediately after you have discovered huge bruises on the arms of a student is not the opportune time to try to discover to whom to report. On the other hand, if the school does not have a policy, certainly the principal should be made aware of the situation. If you are convinced that a case should be reported, either you, the principal, the school nurse, or the school social worker or counselor would be the most likely person to report. Remember, however, that the fact of notifying a superior of your suspicions does not make you personally less liable.

Teachers frequently ask, "What if I report an abusive situation to an administrator who does not feel it should be reported or who feels that there is something wrong with me that I cannot handle the problem myself?" The school administration *should* be involved. A child abuse report is, in effect, based upon the decision of the educational team serving the child. As noted previously, many states consider every school professional a mandated reporter who is therefore responsible. In some cases, administrators may not be familiar with the magnitude of their responsibility in this area or they may feel that reporting will be a reflection upon their school. In fact, reporting a family distress situation points to a school system that is knowledgeable about potential barriers to student learning and concerned about overcoming them. If, however, your administrator will not report and refuses to let you do so, you must make a choice—to try harder to convince the administrator of the severity of the situation, to try to obtain permission to report from the administrator's superior, or to report the situation yourself. (Some states allow anonymous reporting.) Certainly neither of the last two courses of action should be taken without a great deal of thought. But whether the administrator agrees to report or not, two factors still exist: (1) you are legally liable until a report is made, and (2) the child may be in danger. The following was recounted by an extremely distraught and guilt-ridden teacher:

I knew Henry was being beaten by his mother. My colleagues knew it too, and each one had approached our principal individually. Finally, after Henry received a particularly bad beating, I pleaded with the principal to allow me to report. When he flatly refused, I felt I had no recourse. Several days later Henry did not come to school. When I arrived home, my husband greeted me with the evening paper. Henry was dead—a victim of child abuse.

The decision not to report child abuse is not a callous or vindictive one; often it is merely a mistake of judgment. Once an individual knows the consequences of not reporting as well as the procedures for reporting, the decision should be much easier.

One solution to the seemingly overwhelming responsibility of reporting is to have the school policy designate a school team (composed of the school counselor or social worker, nurse, administrators, and teachers, for example) to discuss the potential report and later to provide mutual help in the justification and followup of the report. This method relieves any one teacher of pressure and also offers peer support.

PROTECTIVE AGENCIES

Reporting to the designated protective agency (most often the state or county child welfare agency) usually means a telephone call to give the agency the information necessary to begin an investigation. (See Appendix C.) State law usually requires the following information:

- names of the child and parents

- address
- age and sex of the child
- type and extent of the child's injuries or complaints
- evidence of prior injuries
- explanation of the injuries given by the child
- name and telephone number of the reporter
- actions taken by the reporter (such as detaining the child, photographs)
- other pertinent information.

To this point it has been assumed that the teacher uncovers the abuse. If, however, the child reports to the teacher, it is important to listen in a way that demonstrates your care and concern. Obtain as many facts and details as possible without appearing to conduct an interrogation. Some children may try to swear you to secrecy, yet the fact that they have confided in you is a cry for help. Tell the child sensitively that you must report the situation and why, and do so at the time. For example, you might say, "Daddy needs help. It's not good for him to be doing this to you. I'm afraid you'll get hurt again, and I care about you." Such an explanation is an assurance of your concern not only for the child's welfare, but also for the parent's welfare.

Then, it is important to persuade the child to remain at school while you report the case. If the child goes home immediately after telling you about the situation, there may be several negative results:

1. The child may feel guilty to the point of refuting the story when questioned later. (This is especially likely in cases of sexual abuse.)
2. The child may be subject to further abuse when the parent discovers the disclosure.
3. The child may be fearful of facing the parent and run away from home, resulting eventually in more abuse.

Teachers can usually keep younger children interested in the classroom, giving themselves time to report. If you explain the situation sensitively and carefully to older children, they may agree to wait in the classroom. Needless to say, you should know the exact reporting procedure. You should also tell the agency that the child is at school and urge an immediate response. A note of caution for the concerned teacher: Do not take the child to your own home. Such an act of benevolence may seem to provide the temporary protection the child needs, but it may place you in legal jeopardy. If your state does not give you the legal right to detain a child, you may even be charged with kidnapping. It is better to work within the social service system than to put yourself in a legally precarious position.

If the child refuses to wait, tell the agency and urge immediate action. Social service personnel usually consider such situations to be emergencies so that the agency should be able to act at once. In the meantime, it is important to explain carefully to the child exactly what is happening.

Whether the case is an emergency or not, many states require that a written report follow the oral report within 24 to 72 hours. The school should have the appropriate forms for the written followup. (See Appendix G for a filled-in sample.) This form is sent to the agency designated to receive reports. It may be vital that the agency have this written notification as well as the telephone call in order to begin a thorough investigation. Reporters should be sure, however, to keep a copy of any report they submit for their own and/or the school's records. Of course the information should be kept confidential.

One of the best ways to obtain results on an abuse report is to use documented material—written descriptions of bruises, dates, the accounts of several people, and any other data may be helpful. Legally teachers should not undress a child to discover bruises, but school nurses may have this prerogative. Some school systems have photographed children's bruises. The legality of this practice in a particular state should be carefully checked with the local social service agency. (Also see Appendix E.) Talking with a social worker may also help teachers determine the viability of their reports.

Once the agency receives the report, it determines if there is sufficient evidence to warrant an investigation or, in the case of an emergency, immediate action. This decision or screening process may be completed instantly, or it may take a day or even a week, depending on the emergency nature of the case. A decision to screen in the case means that a social worker or team of social workers will investigate it. Here again, the nature of the case determines how soon action will be taken. Most states mandate an investigation within a week or two, or sooner in an emergency—such as when a child's health is severely threatened or when a delay would cause some immediate danger to the child.

When calling in a report, you may want to ask about the timetable of the agency. You can also assure the social worker of your continued cooperation and ask to be kept informed of the progress of the case. In some states social workers cannot divulge the results of an investigation without the signed affidavit of the alleged abuser, but they may be able to assure you that the case is being investigated. Also, even though some social workers may not keep a reporter informed, many do—especially if they feel that the teacher can continue to be a resource in helping the child and the family.

The important thing to remember at this point is that your report sets in motion the helping process that the family so desperately needs.

Chapter 3

If You Suspect Child Abuse, How Can You Validate Your Suspicion?

As indicated in Chapter 2, each state has its own set of reporting regulations, which may differ considerably from each other. Some states require teachers to report immediately even in cases of suspected abuse or neglect. Other states allow more leeway and expect that cases will be fairly well documented when reported. This chapter offers suggestions to help teachers validate their suspicions of child abuse and thus improve the reporting process. If your state says, "Report even if you only suspect," your sensitivity to validation will enable you to help the social service system either to create a more pressing reason for opening the case, to build a stronger case for court, or to provide additional information to help the social worker work out the best treatment plan. If, on the other hand, your state requires proof of your suspicions, the suggestions provided here will help you supply that proof.

DOCUMENTATION

It is important to have as much information as possible about a situation when reporting. Documentation greatly helps. For example, every time a student comes to class with bruises, jot down the date, the type of bruises, and the child's explanation for them. Also note any contacts you may have had with parents, including their reactions to you as well as their interaction with the child. When you report, or at the time of later court intervention, such documented, factual information will be extremely valuable.

One way to discover more facts about the home situation and to involve parents initially is to treat whatever problem the child exhibits as one that requires special assessment. Through Public Law 94-142, the teacher can request a care evaluation. This consists of a series of tests and assessments focusing on educational needs and describing what the child can or cannot do. It usually culminates in a conference of parents and the professionals concerned with the evaluation. Since the child may also be exhibiting learning difficulties, such an evaluation can be easily justified. Some abuse cases have been handled voluntarily in this way without any court intervention.

ANALYZING DATA

The next step is to analyze your data. For example, for the child who frequently comes to class with bruises, is there anything else about the child's behavior that fits the physical or behavioral clues given in Chapter

1? Have you observed the child and parents together? Do the parents' expectations for the child appear to be too high for a child of that age?

One teacher invites all parents, with their children, for a visit during the school year. At this time she asks each child to demonstrate a task (usually one necessitating adult help), and then she observes any interaction between parent and child. She finds that the interaction gives her invaluable information. As an example, she cites her interview with Danny and his mother.

Mrs. K. greeted me as follows: "I'm not surprised that you have asked me to come in. Now *you* know that Danny is nothing like his older brother, Ed. Ed was so good in school and so cooperative. Then there's Danny!" She indicated the 11-year-old boy standing sullenly behind her. I asked Mrs. K. to sit down and suggested that Danny hang their coats in the back of the room while I got some notes.

"For goodness sakes, Danny! Don't drag my coat," Mrs. K. admonished. "And hang it up right."

Danny did not respond but continued to complete his task "Stand up straight, Daniel," Mrs. K. barked. "It's so tough with these kids," she remarked to me. "Being a mother *and* father is no picnic! In fact, will we be long? I have to pick up my son Ed at a friend's house. Danny, come over here and sit down."

Danny was quietly observing the fish in their tank—moving in endless circles with no hope of escape in their monotonous search for variety in the confines of the tank. Suddenly I saw Danny's life much like that.

Mrs. K.'s further comments made it quite clear to me that no matter what Danny did, he could never meet her expectations. Was the abuse we had observed a symbol of her own frustrations?

Not every teacher has an opportunity to observe either parent or student so closely. At the high school level, a teacher may see the adolescent only for brief class periods. As one instructor noted, "My geometry class is not exactly the arena for sharing feelings. How do *I* know if a child is being abused?" In such situations, teachers need to be observant—that is, aware of peculiar behavior or unusual appearance on the part of the student. Further, they can demonstrate an attitude of openness. A chemistry teacher, for example, in spite of her no-nonsense facts and figures in class inspired students to come to her after class because of her open, accepting attitude. Although high school teachers without home room or advisory responsibilities may not be in a position to report due to lack of information, through observation they may be able to provide valuable support to colleagues who do report.

CONSULTING OTHER PROFESSIONALS

It is important for teachers who suspect abuse or neglect to explore the interactions of their colleagues with the child. Talk with other teachers. Have they noticed these bruises or this behavior? The physical education teacher or the coach, for example, may have noticed bruises as the child changed clothes for gym. If so, you have additional support. It is also important to consult and work with other professionals within the school system. School nurses have the medical expertise to examine bruises, burns, and untreated medical problems. They may be the only ones who have the right to remove a child's clothing; they may also have the right to take photographs of any bruises they uncover. In addition, nurses are in an excellent position to teach the neglected child some basic rules of personal hygiene.

School psychologists are trained not only in testing, which can be helpful in detecting children's problems, but they are also schooled in human motivation and possibly counseling. They may not only help the child through diagnosis and counseling, but may be of help to you as a consultant. School social workers, also trained in counseling, are frequently the professionals most likely to act as links between the child's family and the school, perhaps even making home visits. Valuable information can be gathered from observing the family's attitude toward the child. Are the parents responsive to school intervention? Do they want to help the child or do they see the child as an unwelcome responsibility?

Special education teachers also see a large percentage of child abuse victims. According to a study by James Christiansen, the spelling, math, and reading scores as well as the overall academic achievement of abused children were significantly lower than those of children not subjected to abuse (7). In addition, victims of maltreatment exhibited more psychological and behavioral problems that brought them to the attention of the special education teacher.

Depending upon their size, some schools may or may not have these professionals available, or their duties may be assumed by others. Any careful observer can, in fact, be of help in detecting problems of abuse. In one school, for example, a librarian who has great sensitivity to children and their needs uncovers more cases of maltreatment than any other faculty member. Whatever the school situation, as you attempt to validate your suspicions that a child has been physically abused, neglected, or sexually abused, remember that these colleagues can be of assistance.

In addition to professionals within the school, community agencies that work with abused children can be helpful. Agency representatives can be invited to speak to faculty members about their responsibilities in the reporting procedure. Or individual teachers can make contact with a social worker or supervisor whom they can call to discuss suspicions they may have but do not feel comfortable about reporting. (As a former social worker, I would have much preferred to discuss a case with a teacher than to receive an unsubstantiated report that would later be thrown out, to the frustration of all concerned parties.)

ALTERNATIVE STEPS

A frequent problem for many teachers is student hygiene. For example, a student may come to school very poorly dressed, unkempt, dirty, eliciting complaints from other children about body odor. It is easy to assume that this is a case of blatant neglect. If a child neglect report is filed, however, it may well be screened out when it is discovered that an otherwise loving parent has similar habits of personal hygiene.

This type of situation can provide an example of alternative steps to take before reporting. Poor hygiene is not an uncommon problem, and for the most part it is not life-threatening. You can consult the school nurse and perhaps call the parent in to discuss the case, discreetly and in a nonthreatening, informal way. Sometimes a well-meaning parent who discovers that a child is having difficulty with peers due to an odor problem will gladly attempt to remedy the situation. Or you may uncover concerns about housing, sanitation, or financial need for which the parent can be referred to the appropriate agency.

If, however, after talking with the parent, there appears to be neglect, you will feel more secure about reporting the situation.

COMMUNICATING WITH THE CHILD

As you attempt to validate your concerns about abuse or neglect, your immediate response may be to talk with the child. This may not be advisable for several reasons:

1. The child may be afraid to tell the truth because of—
   - fear of being hurt by the abuser
   - belief that "people go to jail for abuse" (admittedly in some states a jail sentence is a reality, but it is hoped that the child can be helped by a social worker or counselor to deal with this reality)
   - fear that something will happen to him/her (such as removal from the home)
   - loyalty to the parent—no matter how bad the situation may be.
2. The child may feel that the abuse is deserved.

3. While some children may be relieved by the outlet of talking to a sympathetic adult, others may be threatened and withdraw from you.

4. Neglected children may know nothing but neglect.

The best approach is to assure children that you can be approached when they are ready to talk. If a child wants to talk or comes to you to report, listen sensitively, being concerned not only with the youngster's feelings, needs, and comfort, but also with accumulating the data necessary for reporting. Puppet shows, movies, and filmstrips such as *Sometimes It's Okay to Tattle* are useful to show in the classroom. (See Appendix H.) They may elicit reports from children by helping them realize that there is a problem and it is all right to talk about it. For sexual abuse, discussions about the body and each person's right not to be touched without permission can be helpful.

Another method that may inspire a report—especially from young children—is the use of art or play techniques. A classic technique is to ask all the children to draw pictures of themselves and their families. Much can be learned from the activities shown and, in particular, the child's position in the picture. Children frequently speak and draw in metaphors. For example, the physically abused child is often a scapegoat, singled out from siblings. Thus, you may notice that youngsters you suspect of being abused draw pictures depicting themselves as being different or removed in some way from other members of their families. Sexually abused children may be more precise anatomically than other children of their age group. Both sexually abused girls and boys may also draw structures that resemble sexual organs or they may concentrate on intrusive themes (32, 37, 38). Neglected children may have trouble organizing their thoughts or they may use depressed scenes or colors. Since most teachers are not specifically trained in interpreting children's art work, you may wish to consult the school psychologist for an analysis of the content of such drawings. These details are mentioned here to sensitize concerned teachers to material that may be looked at in greater depth.

Although drawing is most frequently associated with younger children, it can be employed with older children in a more symbolic way. For example, "Create a scrapbook or book of drawings about your future. Describe all aspects of your life—your future family, your career, etc." Such an assignment may well uncover the theme "I don't want to do to my kids what my parents did to me!" Older students can also be encouraged to read a book about a family and write a report comparing it with their own.

The validation process may require a few hours or a few weeks, depending upon the potential threat to the child. Neglect and sexual abuse, while potentially destructive, have been continuing for some time. It is better to have clear-cut facts than to report and have the case screened out because of insufficient evidence. Physical abuse, on the other hand, may be life-threatening. Therefore, teachers should report suspected physical abuse as soon as possible. Even in these cases, however, the more factual information you can provide, the more likely it is that something will be done for the child once you have reported.

COMMUNICATING WITH THE PARENTS

If you have concluded that the child is in fact abused or neglected, at what point should you inform the parents? Your first inclination may be to inform the parents that you intend to report. Such an action may pose several problems, however. Consider what may happen in some cases of maltreatment. In neglectful situations the lifestyle may be chaotic and the roots few. A neglectful parent who feels threatened may flee. The same may be true in abuse situations. Mary Jane Chalmers wrote an account of an abusive and neglectful family whose itinerant career prevented detection until it was too late (6).

In addition to flight, there is also the possibility that knowledge of the report may increase the danger to the child, especially if the child is the reporter. Abuse is associated with control—the parent feels desperately out of control and strikes out. The introduction of the social service system or the legal system into the family's life creates an even more vulnerable situation. If the parent feels this threat, the child may in fact suffer more abuse.

Other phenomena operate in cases of sexual abuse. For both victim and perpetrator (especially in cases of incest), there is a higher risk of suicide immediately after a report is made. Once the situation comes to light, the case *must* be handled swiftly and with expert timing.

Certainly the parents must know that the abuse or neglect has been or is to be reported. Social workers differ in their advice as to when to inform the parents, however. Considering the possible parental reactions mentioned, some feel that teachers should report before informing the parents, but that the parents should subsequently be approached by those who are specifically trained to deal with them. Knowledge of such support should be reassuring to teachers.

Other social workers feel that the parents are owed an explanation before the report is made for the following reasons:

1. The situation may be a misunderstanding and once all the parties communicate, a report may be deemed unnecessary.
2. Parents may feel less threatened, more amenable to cooperation, and therefore more willing to seek help if they are approached before the involvement of the social service system. Considering that control is a central issue, especially for abusive parents, it is important to deprive them of as little control as possible.

Because of this difference of opinion among social service personnel concerning parental rights, cooperation, and the child's safety, teachers may want to consult social workers informally for advice.

In some cases, once the report has been made, you may have an opportunity to talk with the child or the parent about the report. But by this time you should have the support of other professionals. Whether or not you see the parent may depend largely on your role in the school and your desire, if any, to further your involvement.

Reporting a child abuse case is not easy for teachers emotionally. Many, although desiring to help the child, feel unsure of their own position and also of the effect the report will have on their future relationship with both child and parents. Some teachers fear repercussions from the family. Physically, the abusive family is dangerous to the child but not usually to adults. Some families may try to "fight back" legally, but teachers who have acted in good faith are legally safe. The worst fear of many educators is that the family may strike out emotionally by making threats to them or false statements to others. However, anyone can be a victim of this type of behavior—from a vindictive neighbor or from a family reported for abuse. The support of colleagues can enable teachers to better handle such annoyances.

I was a new teacher when I encountered Helene's parents. The D.'s were a prominent family who knew all the right people. I suspected that Helene's father was sexually abusing her long before I had the nerve to report it. I talked to several other teachers who finally assured me that reporting was the best thing to do. When the local congressman called my principal, I was panic-stricken. I was sure I would lose my job and my reputation. Fortunately my colleagues supported me, and in time the D.'s received the help they needed. The look in Helene's eyes and her new vitality and interest in school were enough to convince me that I'd done the right thing.

What, then, if the parents withdraw the child from school or from your classroom? This is always a possibility. But at least you will have involved the family members with the social service system so that the child may be helped. If you are able to talk with the parents and assure them that you wish to be an ally, you may be able to help in the treatment.

Remember that abusive families cry for help in a variety of ways and then often erect smokescreens to cover their cries. Many times no one hears until a child is badly harmed or even killed. Classroom teachers may be in a position to hear these cries for help a little sooner than other members of society. You may be the key to early intervention and a turning point in the life of the family.

Certainly reporting child abuse is neither easy nor clear-cut. But the potential benefit for the abused child is worth every effort you are able to expend.

TEACHER'S CHECKLIST FOR PREPARING TO REPORT

1. Have you documented your data and written down the information to organize it in your own mind?
2. Have you analyzed your data? What causes you to suspect abuse/neglect? List the symptons—physical or behavioral.
3. Have you been able to observe the parent/child interaction? Does the parent see the child as worthwhile or different and/or hard tc handle?
4. Have you spoken with other professionals within the school? Do they have reason to suspect abuse/neglect? Why?
5. Do you know the reporting policy of your school? Do you know the answers to the questions on page 32? To whom do you report?
6. Do you have the necessary information required for a report? (See pages 33-34.)
7. Do you (or does the school) have the exact telephone number and address of the agency to which you should report?
8. Have you talked with your administrator about the support you will receive once the report is made? What if the parents try tc remove the child from your class? Will you have the support of the administration?
9. Does your school have on hand the necessary report forms?
10. Have you set up a support system for yourself with other teachers or administrators? (After the report is made, you may feel vulnerable and need to talk.)

Now, you should be ready to report, knowing that you are providing a chance for both the child and the family to receive much-needed help.

Chapter 4

Once You Report, What Happens Then?

After you have made the report and may perhaps be continuing to validate your data, the social service system will have become involved in the case. This chapter answers some of the questions that teachers have about what happens at this point.

PROTECTIVE AGENCY DECISIONS

When a protective investigation begins, the social worker must make several important decisions. These are discussed in the following pages.

Does the Case Warrant Further Intervention?

In some cases, the intervention of the community may promote improvement. At the other extreme, the social worker may receive no cooperation from the parents, yet have insufficient evidence to ensure court involvement. Some parents are well enough acquainted with the social service system to know exactly what to say or how to look, so that when the social worker visits the home, everything appears to be acceptable. In such cases, it is as frustrating for the social worker as it is for the teacher to close a case before rendering any help. Regardless of your frustration, the best course of action is to offer to keep in touch with the agency so that you can share any further developments. It should also be mentioned that some states require the intervention of a law enforcement agency. (See Appendix F.) If this is so in your state, the protective agency will know the role the law enforcement agency plays in these cases. Thus the decisions made on behalf of the child may, in fact, be joint decisions of the two agencies.

Is It Safe for the Child to Remain at Home?

Throughout child welfare history, professionals have vacillated between keeping children in their own home and placing them in a foster home. Children feel greater security in their own home, however dysfunctional it may be. Studies have shown that foster home placement does not necessarily ensure a happier life. In fact, for children who are returned to their own home after foster home placement, the situation may deteriorate faster than it would have without placement.

Although the best plan for the child may seem to be removal from a difficult home situation, the social worker may well decide to have the child remain at home and attempt to work with the family intact. Even in cases of sexual abuse, it is more advisable to remove the perpetrator from the home than the child. Needless to say, the exception would be if the child were in immediate danger. Placements may be made either with the voluntary permission of the parents or by court intervention.

Will the Family Willingly Receive Help?

Families may agree to the intervention of a social worker for several reasons:

- They may sincerely want help and have, in fact, been asking for it by their behavior.
- They may fear the legal consequences if they do not agree to be helped.
- They may comply to "get the social worker off their back."

Whatever the motivation, if the agency feels that the family needs help and the family agrees to cooperate, the relationship will probably be voluntary. While this is the preferred arrangement, it can sometimes be frustrating if the family does not keep appointments or the old problems begin to reappear. If, on the other hand, the family refuses help initially, or at some point decides not to cooperate any longer, the social worker can opt for court involvement.

Particular instances that require court intervention are as follows:

- The child is in imminent danger of harm.
- Attempts at treatment have failed, and parents have not made progress toward providing adequate care for the child. (5, p. 23)

If there is a decision for court intervention, the social worker files a petition in the juvenile division of the civil court requesting that the family be compelled to get help or that the children be placed in a foster home. This sets in motion a series of procedures that are discussed in Chapter 5.

Whether or not there is court involvement or family cooperation, if the case is assessed to need more help, the agency works with the family. At this point you may be asked to give reports to the social worker concerning your contacts with the family or the child's progress in school.

Exactly What Type of Treatment Does the Family Need?

Family treatment may take several forms:

- concrete services such as financial assistance, medical assistance housing assistance, day care (to relieve the parent of some stress)
- referral to other services specific to family needs, such as services for special children, family planning, budgeting consultation, counseling

- advocacy services—helping the family to actually obtain the services for which it is eligible
- counseling services (most protective agencies are able to provide these in a limited way; if more in-depth counseling is needed, the family is referred to another source).

Who Will Be Involved in the Treatment of the Family?

The group of professionals concerned with the assessment or treatment of protective situations is often referred to as the Child Protection Team. Some teams are involved only in assessment; others meet for progress reports on the family throughout the treatment. Whether or not there is a formal network, the social worker may involve all or some of the following: health professionals, the child's teacher(s) and perhaps the school nurse, the school social worker, a psychologist, a psychiatric social worker, legal services and other support personnel (from welfare, day care, etc.) as needed, and possibly the child's foster parents, if placement has been indicated. It is most important that all the links of this therapeutic chain remain in contact with one another, bearing in mind that the primary goal is to help the family. Some families may be skillful in building mistrust between professionals. An interesting novel, *The Scofield Diagnosis*, deals with a doctor's attempt to help an abusive family amidst the barriers set up by other professionals (11). Some families may also misinterpret information; as a result mistrust can be built between agencies.

How Long Will Treatment Take?

This is difficult to answer. Many social service agencies set up treatment plans with clients ranging from weeks to months. If the court becomes involved, it may schedule hearings at regular intervals, from six weeks to six months. The severity of the situation may also determine the length of treatment. If the family's prognosis is very poor and few gains are made, the children may be removed. If, on the other hand, the family appears workable, more time may be spent on teaching more effective parenting skills. No abuse or neglect situation can be remedied immediately. The deterioration of family life did not happen overnight.

At What Point Does the Family No Longer Need Services?

The obvious answer depends on the type of child maltreatment:

- In physical abuse, services are terminated when the abuser stops abusing the child and has learned another method of coping with aggressive feelings.
- In neglect, services are terminated when the parent can meet the child's basic needs adequately.

46

- In sexual abuse, services are terminated when the perpetrator is no longer involved sexually with the child and, ideally, has learned more coping methods to prevent such involvement in the future.

These answers are all that society can realistically offer in these cases, and unfortunately it is difficult to determine if the gains made will be lasting. Some social agencies have arbitrary time limits based upon restrictions of staff time and agency funds. If there is court involvement the case continues until no further evidence indicates abuse.

Few professionals who work with these families are pleased with the criteria used for closing their cases. But until humans become more skilled in understanding and determining human motivation, these are the criteria they must use.

Chapter 5

What If You
Have to Go to Court?

The first time it was necessary for me to go to court in a juvenile matter, I was apprehensive. I expected to see Perry Mason in all his glory; what I did see was a small courtroom—not unlike a formal classroom—with only a handful of people in attendance.

Family or juvenile court sessions are closed with only the legal staff and the significant people present. No observers may attend and if, in fact, you are asked to serve as a witness, you may be asked to leave the room after your testimony is given.

SUGGESTIONS FOR A COURT APPEARANCE

Your chances of going to court are probably not very great, but it is best to be prepared if you are asked to appear. Protective cases are taken to court if the social worker feels that either the child is in real danger or the family will not cooperate. Prior to any court hearing, the social service agency (or police) files a petition stating that the child is in need of the court's protection. Also, there may be a pretrial hearing to determine if the case can be resolved without court intervention, or if in fact there is enough evidence to go to court. The social service agency then must collect witnesses to substantiate the report. At this point, you may receive a subpoena. In the courtroom there will be no jury, merely a judge, court officers, probation officers, lawyers (for parents, for child, and perhaps for the social service agency), social service personnel, and witnesses. You will merely be asked to state your involvement and any information you may have about the case. One teacher recounts her experience in court and makes some recommendations:

As a teacher, I had the opportunity to be a witness in a child neglect hearing. It is very important to bring documentation with you to the hearing. This may include test scores; observations of home conditions; parent and child behavior within the home, and clinical and classroom settings; photographs and dates of home and school contacts. Try to answer each question as truthfully as you can, as you are under oath. In my case, I included not only negative aspects of home conditions and parenting skills, but also positive aspects of the home environment. I answered only when spoken to and did not give my personal opinion on any of the questions asked me.

When testifying, do not sound defensive. As a witness, you are not being judged and you need not fear being interrogated. In my particular situation I was briefed several weeks in advance of the hearing as to the types of questions I might be asked in the courtroom and I was not allowed to hear the other witnesses' testimony during the hearing. If the witnesses are not notified of the results of the hearing, they should contact the social worker involved in the case or the lawyer who is the custodian of the children involved. These professionals should give you the information you want, respecting the rights of confidentiality of all those involved.

In addition to these suggestions, it may also be helpful—

- to dress appropriately—considering that courts are conservative.
- to prepare ahead—the documentation of fact, dates, etc., will help you remember.
- not to memorize your testimony—it should sound spontaneous. (5, pp. 49-50)

You may feel somewhat nervous; most people usually do, especially when asked to take an oath. Preparing yourself mentally to answer and concentrating on speaking both loudly and clearly will help (5, pp.50-51).

The court will be recording your testimony, so it is important that it be clearly audible. If you don't know the answer, don't guess; say you don't know. Although you may be separated from other witnesses, in some cases you may hear their testimony. It is important to present your own story in an organized manner, and to be unafraid to admit your own beliefs.

In some situations you may be asked to appear at a later hearing to update the court on the progress of the child. More than likely, however, you will need to make only one appearance.

Finally, no matter how many times you are asked to appear in court, it should not give you undue anxiety if you remember that you are not on trial. You are merely there to help the child.

Chapter 6

What Can You Do for the Child, Beyond Reporting?

COMMUNICATING WITH THE SOCIAL WORKER

Once child abuse has been reported, the two most important professionals in the child's life are the social worker and the teacher. It is therefore vital that these two key figures work together. Both the social worker who does not consult the teacher and the teacher who does not keep in touch with the social worker miss important information that can help the child as well as each other.

Some teachers have said, "What's the point of reporting? I never heard a thing from the social worker and obviously nothing was done." Not unlike teachers who attempt to give of themselves with skill and understanding to their classes of 30 youngsters, social workers, too, have very large caseloads. Often their attention goes—by necessity—from crisis to crisis with insufficient time for the details of any one case. The neophyte social worker may feel overwhelmed; the overworked, experienced social worker may appear mechanical. But remaining in this profession requires a sincere concern for the welfare of one's clients.

"I may not always get back to teachers as I should," admits an experienced social worker, "but I really appreciate a phone call letting me know how the child is doing or if anything new has come up with the child or the family."

Although the social worker may be making the major decisions in the child's life, it is the teacher who "lives" with the child day after day whose information can be vital to an agency's treatment plan. Of course the decisions of the social worker are influenced not only by agency policy but also by the court system. A child may be returned to a natural family not because the social worker feels it is the best plan, but because of insufficient evidence for the court to continue custody. In some cases careful documentation by the teacher has been the factor that enabled the social worker and the court to provide a better treatment plan for a child when everyone was convinced that the case should be dismissed.

This is not meant to imply that the responsibility for communication should be solely the teacher's. It is mutual. Both professionals complain of finding it difficult to contact each other. However, most social workers have a day in their offices when they can be reached more easily. And teachers can let social workers know when they have a free period and can be more easily reached by telephone.

HELPING THE CHILD INDIVIDUALLY

Over the years it becomes clear that abuse and neglect take their toll on a variety of children, usually in similar ways. Abused or neglected children may—

- have a very poor self-image, feeling that they do not matter or that there is something wrong with them.
- need individual attention.
- need to express frustration and anger.
- have unattended educational or medical needs.
- need to succeed—to do something right.
- need to know that they have rights too; those with poor self-image may not know that it is all right to say no to adults.
- have hampered development emotionally, physically, or sexually.

Some types of assistance for these children are obvious. Referrals for medical testing within the school as well as assessment for special learning needs can be made for any child. Perhaps the two biggest needs—both related—of maltreated children are to improve the self-image and to do "something right." There is also the need to express anger at what has been done to them. Any tasks or exercises that can meet these needs can be helpful. For example, choose tasks that give the youngster a feeling of authority in the classroom or on the playground—something as simple as erasing the chalkboard. Or choose caretaking tasks such as feeding the gerbils. This enables the child to be the caregiver and to learn ways to properly care for something or someone as well as to feel important. And a quiet word of approval upon completion of the task may mean a great deal to the abused or neglected child. It is of course important to rotate key tasks so that one child does not seem to be favored.

High school students can also be given tasks of importance. In each class, the teacher has an opportunity to comment on the student's little successes as they are accomplished. For some older children, the sports area is a natural outlet. Shooting a few baskets amidst quips about life and happenings at school may be the perfect occasion for building trust by encouraging the youngster to focus on the positive or attainable elements of his or her life.

The high school years also provide an excellent opportunity to help students assess their strengths in the interest of career goals—with coaxing perhaps from a guidance counselor, a concerned teacher, or a coach. Several programs are available to help teens not focused on college—either because of financial reasons, lack of motivation, or self-concept—assess and prepare themselves for some type of job. These programs—such as Jobs for America's Graduates (1750 Pennsylvania Ave., NW,

Washington, DC 20006)—not only help students explore strengths and weaknesses, they also train them in resume writing, job searching, interviewing, and getting along with others in a work setting. Such skills can be invaluable to a child whose emotional growth and ambition may have been stunted by abuse and neglect.

The high school years seem to be the time when many young people are looking for a mentor. Perhaps one of the greatest benefits the teacher can offer those in this age group, other than helping them discover themselves, is to be open and approachable as a person—that is, to communicate that you will hear them if they need to talk.

A high school teacher enrolled in my "Sexual Abuse" course carried her text to school, at first unwittingly, intending to read it during her study period. Many students never noticed the book, but several who did asked questions and eventually were able to talk with her regarding abuse they had suffered. Besides making referrals to help these youngsters, this teacher was able to stand by her students in a way that told them that she was there if they needed her again.

Some students, teens or younger, are not so easily helped. The behavior of disruptive children may need to be dealt with firmly, but with increased understanding. Unfortunately the school's frequent disciplinary tool is suspension, one of the worst things that could happen to an abused or neglected child. And the use of corporal punishment—already prohibited in several states and discouraged in most others—is also highly undesirable for these children. A more effective method is to point out the positive benefits of acceptable behavior, at the same time motivating the children to accept responsibility for their actions and also to feel deserving of any rewards that may result. For a good illustration of this technique in use, see *Marva Collins' Way,* the story of an educator with a real skill in getting through to children considered problems (8, p. 20).

Children who have been abused need to feel that they have alternatives and the rewards of their choices. Or, whether destructive or withdrawn, they may just need time to talk about what has happened to them. The informed teacher can be their best ally. Understanding through reading and/or training what has happened to the child can be of invaluable help in knowing what to say. Sensitivity to clues that the child needs to talk— such as a change of behavior or attitude—is important.

Certain exercises can give children an opportunity to share their feelings. For example, "On My Mind" encourages students to draw silhouettes of themselves and then "cut out words, pictures, etc., that represent their personal thoughts, thus making a collage of their current concerns" (40). This type of exercise not only gives children an opportunity to express feelings or concerns, but it helps them realize that their feelings *are* important. In addition, teachers of younger children can use puppets or other toys to enable youngsters to voice their own feelings.

HELPING THE CHILD IN THE CLASSROOM

The average teacher may not have time for more individual help or may not want to single out a child. It is possible, however, to help the abused or neglected child within the classroom with resulting benefit to the whole class. Such help can accomplish several purposes:

- It enhances the self-image and feelings of worth not only of the abused or neglected child, but of classmates as well.
- It enables classmates to understand the abused or neglected child.
- It stimulates other reports and educates children in areas relating to abuse and neglect.

The type of exercise used in the classroom may be general or specific. For example, all children may participate in an activity designed to enhance self-image or they may view a film geared specifically toward preventing abuse or encouraging the reporting of abuse.

Enhancing Self-Image and Feelings of Worth

Wells and Canfield cite numerous exercises, many of which can help a child feel important. They use such topics as "My Strength," "Who Am I?" "Accepting My Body," and "Where Am I Going?" to help the child develop a better concept of self (40). Other exercises in this area include discussions such as "What's the Best Thing About Me?" or in the case of high-school-age students, "What Have I Accomplished About Which I Am Most Proud?" These discussions are good ways not only to discern the quality of the individual's self-image, but also to help improve it. Class projects in which all members have a part are also useful to help children feel needed.

Other helpful books include *Personalizing Education: Values Clarification and Beyond* (22), *Teaching Children to Love Themselves* (27), and *Left-Handed Teaching: Lessons in Affective Education* (4).

How else can you help the child in class? Use any activity that encourages children to think in terms of their own potential rather than of their limitations. Such exercises can help both abused and neglected children and their classmates think more of themselves. Or begin in another way. Even though it may be difficult with some children, look for their positive attributes or strengths. A mental exercise searching out these strengths may be good with a particular child who may be especially trying or unpopular with other students.

Once you have a sense of the positive aspects of this child, encourage them. Granted, if in a class of 30 children you begin to accentuate the

53

positive aspects of one abused or neglected child, the remainder of the class may react. You may therefore want to acknowledge the strengths of all the children, enlisting their help to discover their own strengths in the form of a game, for example. (Several such games are listed in the books just mentioned.) Or first ask the children to think about the "good things" about themselves. Keep in mind that children with poor self-images may have difficulty identifying positive points about themselves and may need gentle coaxing or suggestions. The fact that an adult, especially an authority figure, is able to see that they do anything well may be the first step toward increased trust between you and these children and may perhaps begin to move them toward the development of a better self-image.

Sometimes you can ask students to write autobiographies, and through this means help them recognize the positive aspects of their lives as well as of themselves. For a child whose life story is punctuated with pain, there can always be positives if one looks for them. For example, Robbie (mentioned in Chapter 1 as a neglected child) was becoming aware that he received little of his parents' attention. Yet as a caretaker of younger siblings, he could be helped to realize his great importance to them. It might also be helpful to emphasize to Robbie how responsible it is of him to come to school every day. Admittedly in such a case you would be overlooking negatives—such as the possible stealing, the hygiene—but as you began to improve Robbie's image of himself, you would have his trust and attention in teaching the class about hygiene, for example, or arranging a school lunch for him, or teaching him to make lunch himself if any supplies were available at home.

Remember that abused and neglected children probably live in a world of negatives at home. Emphasizing their positive aspects may be difficult for them to handle at first, but with practice, the effect may even transfer into the home.

It is perhaps more difficult to help the high school student in the classroom setting because of the constantly changing environment—class membership, subject, etc. Some subjects, however, lend themselves to self-exploration and enhancement of self-image. For example, you can use a literature course to look at the role of women in literature, emphasizing not only the author's message, characterization, and plot, but also the strengths portrayed by women. This can lead to an opportunity to help the female (and perhaps male) class members assess their own strengths. Health or family life courses can lead more obviously to looking at the self and individual potential. Peer support groups are another vehicle to help teens with adolescent/self-image issues. Adolescence, a natural period of self-exploration, can prove a perfect time to introduce positive concepts and role models.

Helping Classmates Understand the Abused or Neglected Child

Children find it difficult to understand why a particular child disrupts a classroom or antagonizes peers. Even more incomprehensible to the more outgoing child is the quiet, withdrawn student who seems removed from the classroom environment. The way in which the abused or neglected child chooses to deal with peers may greatly affect the peers' responses.

Perhaps a starting point is to educate the class about feelings, emotions, and even abuse, including the feelings that an abused person may have. This can be done simply by presenting "What-if" statements to which children respond. For example, "What if a friend breaks your. favorite toy?" or "What if your mother hits you very hard?" Once children explore the range of possible feelings in response to these statements, they will be able to better understand the feelings of others.

In the case of children who are withdrawn, you might encourage other students to include them in their games. Making such a request of a more outgoing or empathetic child may prove the most successful.

If children are disruptive, the chances are they are disturbing their classmates. Students will frequently handle the situation themselves if given a chance, but a lesson in empathetic response can change the "Aw, keep still, Johnny!" to "You're a nice kid, and I hate to see you have everyone mad at you by . . ." Children respond to their environment. They will imitate the teacher who employs an empathetic approach.

Hygiene problems can also be handled by peers. In one case a high school student patiently counseled a peer on the need for bathing to acquire more friends. A few years ago, the norm was "the dirtier the better" but the importance of designer jeans somehow emphasizes a clean body. Thus cleanliness can help students feel more acceptable.

The high school student whose primary goal is to be "one of the gang" may find it more difficult to step away from the crowd and help a peer. If a benevolent student cannot be found, peer support groups set up by the guidance office can sometimes be useful in communicating acceptance to an otherwise outcast teenager. Again, education can be the key. Teenagers may be more empathetic if they perceive the reason for a classmate's problem.

Stimulating Other Reports

There are a variety of ways to encourage reporting. Specific filmstrips such as *Sometimes It's Okay to Tattle* and *Some Secrets Should be Told* talk to younger children about abuse and sexual abuse. *Child Abuse: Don't Hide the Hurt* discusses latency for preteens. *Who Do You Tell?* prepares children (7 to 12 years of age) for reporting abuse and also aids them in knowing where to go in other emergencies. (See Appendix H.)

In addition, there are training programs geared to personal safety and prevention of sexual abuse. These programs address a variety of developmental issues such as privacy and assertiveness as well as abuse. Books for children such as *Red Flag, Green Flag People* or *My Very Own Book About Me* can be used as workbooks to aid students' understanding of how to prevent sexual abuse. Such tools may also stimulate reports. (See Appendix H.)

As a way of understanding, educating, and encouraging reports, children can be asked to write puppet shows or plays telling about abuse. One sixth grade class, with help from a local social agency, wrote a play on what to do if a friend is abused. Then the class presented it to the school. The result was overwhelming. The door was opened. Not only was the class better informed, but other children within the school felt better able to self-report.

Here, too, it may be helpful to educate children in issues relating to abuse and neglect such as hygiene. For years advertisers of toothpastes and soaps have made their products more appealing by animation and dramatization. Some free programs may be available through these companies for classroom use, or all the children can do a project on hygiene to create more sensitivity in the entire group and to prevent any one child from being singled out.

Sex education is an area fraught with controversy. Is it the responsibility of the parent or the school? The fact is that many children have much misinformation about sexual concepts. Surprisingly, sexually abused children may be equally misinformed. They may have been taken beyond their years in sexual activity but lack knowledge of normal experience. In addition, children need to be taught about their bodies in general, with emphasis on appreciating them.

A variety of other topics can also help abused and neglected children and their classmates. A quick perusal of the symptoms listed in Chapter 1 may bring more of these to mind.

HELPING THE FOSTER CHILD IN THE CLASSROOM

Foster children may need a special kind of concern from their teachers. You may find in your classroom a student who has been removed from home for protective reasons and lives in a foster home. This child may present special problems. The biggest issue that the foster child is probably working out is that of separation and loss. No matter how difficult the home situation, this child has experienced the loss of an important element of life. The expression of this loss may differ from individual to individual. One child may be withdrawn or sullen, another difficult, exhibiting behavior problems. Feelings of inconstancy and instability may create a child who seems not to care. The best way to deal with these situations is to contact the social worker and insist on being told something of the child's background. The youngster may have special needs or interests that you can address. Mostly, however, foster children are wondering if you will reject or abandon them as others seem to have done. They may test you or tell wild, unbelievable stories to shock you. Knowledge of their background may help here too. The need to know that they are all right, no matter what the family situation, is paramount for these youngsters. Again the classroom teacher can be not only an ally, but also an important source of information on the child's progress by maintaining close contact with the social worker and the foster parents.

Any discussion of help for foster children would be remiss without mentioning the importance of the foster parents. These people as a group may be victims of misconceptions. The vast majority, greatly overworked and grossly underpaid, are concerned, dedicated individuals who take their job seriously. As one foster mother put it:

When a child is placed in a foster home, the foster parents take on many roles. . . . The formal professional role of the child protective team is essential but the informal daily role of the foster parent is at the root of the child's progress. It is the foster parent who makes the majority of appointments, who must screen the child for possible problems, with resulting treatments afer discussions and consultation with professional staff. Bypassing the foster parent's role in the treatment of the "trauma of child abuse and neglect" is like bypassing the electrical outlet in the operation of any electrical apparatus. The foster parent is the link between the many forces involved in this endeavor.

Frequent contact with the foster parents can help the teacher understand what is happening in the child's homelife and provide them with information concerning the child's progress in school. Through the foster parents the teacher can learn of any new treatments that may have altered the child's behavior in the school setting. A note, a telephone call, or an appointment with these caretakers can ensure the more harmonious orchestration of the child's already out-of-tune life.

Whether keeping in touch with the child's natural or surrogate parents, aiding the social service team, or daily contacts in the classroom, the influence of the teacher on an abused or neglected child is profound. In many cases the teacher is the second most influential person in the child's life—one whose membership on the treatment team is vital.

Chapter 7

Who Is
the Child's Family?

Current newspapers and magazines are full of statistics attesting to the "vicious maltreatment of children by their parents." Yet the sensationalistic drama of these statistics distorts the picture of the distraught human being behind the abuse. Admittedly, teachers who see the evidence of child abuse and neglect find it difficult to imagine that anyone could relate to children in such ways. However, except for an inability to deal with life in cases of extremes, the parents of these child victims are not unlike other people.

This chapter contains profiles of the physically abusive parent, the neglectful parent, the sexually abusive parent, and the emotionally abusive parent. Individual parents may not fit these profiles exactly. But in most cases enough of the characteristics are usually present so that teachers can use these guidelines for recognition.

THE PHYSICALLY ABUSIVE PARENT

Libby Carter was a neat, well-dressed young woman whose house appeared immaculate—to the few who had seen it. Libby, her husband, and two children had recently moved and she reported knowing few people. Deeper exploration of Libby's family background would have revealed that she had married young and had had an extremely difficult time in her pregnancies, especially with Tommy, her first child. As a baby, Tommy had been colicky and difficult, and Libby, an only child, had felt at a loss to know what to do. Her husband, Mike, a hard-working, conservative man, expected her to know what to do. He frequently brought work home and was annoyed when Tommy's crying made it difficult to concentrate. In addition, the couple never seemed to be able to make ends meet, which caused a great deal of friction between the two.

This may not seem to be an unusual scenario in an age of unpredictable economy and increased mobility. However, Libby Carter was brought to the attention of the local protective agency because five-year-old Tommy repeatedly came to school with unexplained bruises.

Any parent will readily admit that there are times when a child becomes so exasperating that it may be difficult not to lash out in anger.

Most parents, however, are able to maintain control so that they do not abuse their children or punish them excessively. Somewhere they have learned how to maintain control. Dr. Ray Helfer described physically abusive individuals as those whose experiences with their own parents have not provided adequate preparation to become parents themselves. In short, they have not learned five vital elements.*

1. Abusive parents have not learned appropriate ways to have their needs met.

Helfer use the scenario of the child who asks a question while the parent is on the ¬lephone. The parent continues the conversation and the child becomes more insistent. Instead of simply answering, "I'll be with you in a minute," the parent continues to ignore the child until the request becomes a tantrum. Then the parent responds. Eventually the child learns to do away with the earlier steps and just has the tantrum. As an adult this translates into overreactions in order to have needs met.

2. Abusive parents have not learned the difference between feelings and actions.

If a parent consistently strikes out in anger rather than verbalizing the anger, the child learns that anger equals aggression or hitting. As an adult this individual may hit when angry instead of recognizing the anger and treating it in a different way.

3. Abusive parents have not learned to make decisions.

It stands to reason that if control is an issue in abusive situations, the abuser feels out of control. Most parents give their children chances to make decisions without even thinking about it: "Would you like peanut butter and jelly or bologna in your lunchbox tomorrow?" Children whose lives are so thoroughly structured that they are not allowed to make any decisions begin to feel powerless and this feeling may transfer into later life.

Helfer also pointed out that children should be given opportunities to make decisions appropriate to their role. For example, it is not so much "Do you want to go to bed?" as "Which foot would you like to put on the stair first, on your way to bed?"

4. Abusive parents have not learned that they are responsible for their own actions and not for the actions of others.

Have you ever known a child whose parent communicates in grief and bitterness that an absent spouse (perhaps too immature to handle the

---

*These tasks were discussed in a lecture given by Dr. Helfer, in New Bedford, Mass., in March 1979. They are adapted with permission.

problems of parenting) would not have left the home if it had not been for the child? In such cases the child begins to feel responsible for the pain others are experiencing.

At the same time, if not taught otherwise, the child may begin to deny responsibility for deeds or misdeeds. The classic response of the two- or three-year-old, "The dog did it," become internalized so that as an adult the individual feels powerless and becomes convinced that whatever the offense, it was in fact caused by the action of another.

5. Abusive parents have not learned to delay gratification.

Children naturally want instant satisfaction of their desires. But as they are guided through development, they come to realize that some pleasures must be delayed. Adults who have not learned this lesson want instant results—immediate obedience from their children or immediate solutions to their problems. When the act or solution does not ensue directly, the individual feels out of control and may react negatively.

Parents who have not learned these tasks in their own childhood may not teach them to their offspring. Thus there is a pattern—many abusive parents were themselves abused as children. This is not to say that every maltreated child will become an abusive adult. One of the keys to interrupt the cycle seems to be insight and learning these identified tasks in later life. Helfer also contends that the learning of these tasks should be a necessary part of any treatment program. His *Childhood Comes First: A Crash Course in Childhood for Adults* was written to help parents learn these tasks (20).

In addition to inadequate preparation for parenting, environmental factors may play a part in the drama of abuse. Often physically abusive parents may experience the following:

- frequent geographic moves
- financial stresses such as uncertain employment, changes in employment, or underemployment
- other types of stresses.

Also at high risk are parents in situations that include

- marriage at a very young age
- pregnancy before or shortly after marriage
- difficult labor and delivery
- abusive families during their own childhood
- marital difficulties.

In short, the lives of abusive parents are characterized by a great many stresses. The parents themselves usually present a picture of

- social isolation

- excessive neatness
- unrealistically high expectations for children
- role reversal with children (i.e., the child parents tne parent and often does a great many parental tasks such as housework and child care)
- poor control of children (especially older children)
- inability to cope with crises.

Unusually high expectations can be seen frequently in abusive families. Parents look to their offspring as extensions of themselves and as somehow responsible for proving that they are worthwhile. Failure to meet parental expectations convinces the children that they are of little worth—a feeling which with ripple effect creates a feeling of failure in the parents as well. The diagram of the vicious cycle of physical abuse depicts this self-perpetuating phenomenon.

Adolescent Abuse

Adolescent abuse may, in some instances, differ from the abuse of younger children. And the motivations of the parents, in turn, may differ as well. There are three types of adolescent abuse:

1. Abuse that begins in childhood and continues through adolescence
2. Abuse that may begin in childhood, such as spankings, but intensifies in adolescence
3. Abuse that begins in adolescence and is directly related to the problems of adolescence. (14, p. 5)

The first type of adolescent abuse is based on too high, unmet parental expectations. Because these unrealistic expectations are not being met, the parents feel that they are failures as parents. The abuse that is perpetrated against a young child up to 7 years of age may let up slightly during the otherwise quiet latency years (7 to 11) but may be stimulated again during the turbulent teens. Thus there is a pattern of continuing, though fluctuating, abuse.

The second type of adolescent abuse is related to control. During childhood the family accepts and uses corporal punishment, which appears to compel the child into acceptable behavior. As the child grows in stature and independence, however, this type of punishment is ineffective. At the same time, the older parent begins to feel more and more out of control of the situation and abuse ensues.

This abusive behavior intensifies in adolescence. While the young child could be subdued by threats over control or belittlement, the adolescent tests, to the point that the parent feels that only physical means will suffice. Emotions by this time have usually reached a fever pitch and abuse is the outcome.

VICIOUS CYCLE OF PHYSICAL ABUSE

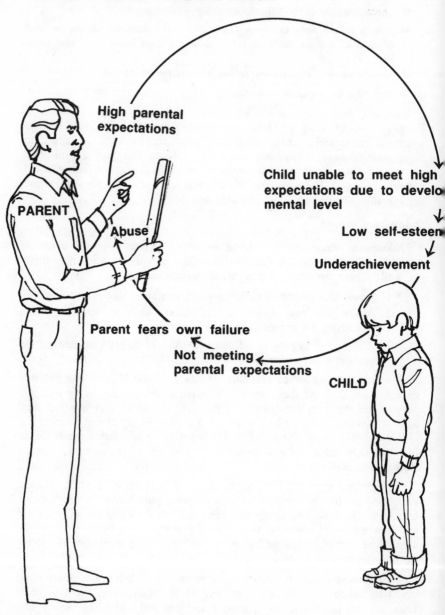

High parental expectations

PARENT

Abuse

Child unable to meet high expectations due to developmental level

Low self-esteem

Underachievement

Parent fears own failure

Not meeting parental expectations

CHILD

The third type of adolescent abuse becomes obvious in the following:

Mary had been a model child and an excellent student just as her mother before her had been. Mary's mother, who was remembered by some of the older teachers in the small town school, had had a brilliant school career and had gone on to college, eventually marrying later in life. An only child, Mary had always been doted upon by her parents. Now in high school, her popularity was assured by her open, jovial manner. She was quite confident and appeared very much her own person. At the beginning of her junior year, however, the teachers were much surprised by the change in Mary. She became sullen, difficult, and verbally abusive to peers and teachers alike. So concerned was the school counselor that she asked Mary's parents to come to school. Sensing a definite change in the family atmosphere, the counselor asked that the family seek outside counseling. The counseling eventually revealed that Mary's mother, once an outgoing, popular girl like her daughter, was feeling emotionally unsupported and worthless. Watching her daughter's beauty and sexuality wax as her own waned became too much for this insecure woman. Feeling totally out of control of the situation, she struck out at Mary who, in her distorted view, appeared as the cause of her turmoil.

While an adolescent is blossoming into adulthood, the parent may be looking forward only to retirement, seeing her or his life being lived again through the child and yet feeling powerless to control it. This period has been called "change of life" and sometimes "middlescence," denoting the adult in midyears battling the same identity issues as the adolescent offspring, with perhaps not as much to look forward to. Fisher, et al. cite three family patterns in which parents are working through issues at the same time as their children:

1. Abuse may be related to the working through of the developmental issue of sexuality. The father may be aroused by his daughter's blossoming, feel guilty and reject or strike out against his daughter. He may also project his guilt upon her boyfriends, accusing them of taking advantage of his daughter. The same pattern may operate with mothers and their sons. Uncontrolled, these feelings could escalate to abuse.

2. Abuse may be related to fears about separation. Parents who dote on their children in childhood may not be prepared for the turbulence of adolescence. Sporadic incidents of testing behavior, as the teen attempts to explore independence, may provoke abuse. Frequently the adolescent feels forced into making a drastic break from the family setting (running away, for example).

63

3. Abuse may be a result of the parents' needs to work through their own unresolved adolescent issues. Parents feeling in competition with the child may participate in peer-like fights.

The rivalry may even take on overtones of sexuality, as between daughter and divorced mother. The adolescent may also be "set up" to act out against authority figures as the parent never dared. Parents feeling conflict over their own inner pulls and their son or daughter's behavior may respond to the child abusively. (14, pp. 40-41)

Whatever the family dynamics, this type of adolescent abuse results from the conflict between the developmental stages of adolescence and middlescence.

Abusive parents of young children or adolescents are fearful of disclosure and racked with guilt. They fear censure and often have nowhere to turn. In the life of the average, relatively happy, individual, friends and a social life are an integral part of everyday experience. More often than not, the abusive parent lacks these contacts and has few friends to turn to in a crisis. This parent does not have a support system and thus feels isolated, alone, and unable to function in a healthy way.

Unfortunately the problems of abusive parents may have repercussions. Their inability to handle emotions appropriately may be transferred to older offspring. It is not unusual to find a teenager who reflects such parental behavior by abusing a younger sibling.

It should also be noted that some apparent examples of parental abuse may not be what they seem. As pointed out in the discussion of physical abuse in Chapter 1, some children exhibit evidence of certain cultural customs that appear to be indicators of abuse or neglect. Awareness of cultural differences and careful observation can help teachers distinguish between these two situations.

The importance of this distinction is demonstrated by a 1983 ruling by the Maryland Court of Special Appeals:

In this case a child newly arrived in the United States from the Central African Republic was placed in a foster home after county officials, investigating doctors' reports of scars on the child's body, decided she was a victim of child abuse. The child's father insisted that his daughter's wounds resulted from cuts from the tall, sharp grasses common to his country and from a doctor's use of a heated cow's horn to treat the cuts.

In its ruling, the intermediate appellate court decided: "There is a serious question whether the evidence in this case warrants so drastic a disposition as to have removed [the child] from her home. . . . There was not the slightest evidence that the parents, either of them, had abused the child."

THE NEGLECTFUL PARENT

The neglectful parent shares certain characteristics with the abusive parent such as poor self-image and role reversal with the child. In other areas, there are marked differences. While almost compulsive order and cleanliness may characterize the life of the abusive parent, the life of the neglectful parent is practically devoid of routine or consistency, and issues such as cleanliness have little import.

The overwhelming desire of neglectful parents is to meet their unmet needs, which are tragic remnants of their own childhood neglect. The most obvious characteristic of these individuals is a lack of constructive energy. They may be apathetic or hostile, and appear to lack the ability to parent constructively.

Neglectful parents may or may not have a support system. For those who do, however, it is often a deviant subculture of other neglectful parents.

According to Polansky, Chalmers, Buttenweiser, and Williams, theorists have attributed neglect to a variety of causes:

. . . the economic, emphasizing the role of material deprivation and poverty; the ecological,* in which a family's background is seen as responsive to the larger social context in which it is embedded; and the personalistic, which attributes poor child care to individual differences among parental personalities, particularly their character structures. (33, p.21)

The authors of this study (which emphasized mothers because fathers were not always available) lean toward the personalistic or developmental failures in parents. They cited several parental subcategories, including "apathetic-futile, impulse-ridden, mentally retarded women in reactive depression, women who are borderline psychotic" (33, p. 38). Social workers work with numerous clients whom these authors described as "women who appeared passive, withdrawn, lacking in expression" (33, p. 39). In addition, these women were characterized by:

- a feeling that nothing was worth doing (for example, "What's the point of changing the baby's diaper, he'll only wet it again?")
- an emotional numbness or lack of affect that may be mistaken for depression
- superficial relationships where the needy individual desperately clings to another
- a lack of competence in basic daily living skills compounded by a fear of failure if they tried to learn these skills
- a passive expression of anger through hostile compliance

---

*Ecological refers to social context in relation to degenerating neighborhoods, etc., which attract people with similar lifestyles.

- a general negative attitude
- a hampered ability to problem solve, making verbal accessibility to others difficult
- a perhaps unconscious ability to make others feel as negative and depressed as they do. (33, pp. 39-40)

Consider the following example:

Mrs. Benner was a 25-year-old mother of five children: Ralphie, 6 years; Eddie, 3 years; Susan, 20 months; and twins, Terry and Gerry, 6 months. The Benner family was reported by Ralphie's teacher who was concerned about his rotting teeth, extremely dirty appearance, and the fact that he appeared to have a good deal of child care responsibility despite his age. Shortly after the report, the twins were hospitalized for malnutrition.

The Benner house was in extremely poor condition with a strong smell of urine and little visible evidence of food. Mrs. Benner greeted the school social worker in a torn, dirty housecoat and although she talked, she had an aura of passive hostility. Susan was standing at the bars in a nearby crib, clad only in a soiled undershirt. When asked why the baby was not diapered, Mrs. Benner responded that she'd only have to be changed. The crib sheet was torn and had been urinated upon numerous times.

Although Mrs. Benner was apparently highly dependent upon her live-in boyfriend, their relationship consisted of watching TV and frequenting the local pub—leaving Ralphie to care for the other children. Mrs. Benner had little sense of housekeeping or child care and no idea of how to use the food she received from the community agency. Any attempts to help her cook creatively with this food or to clean and care for her children were met with a sullen response of noncompliance. Only the threat of the children's removal eventually elicited some positive response.

In addition to the Polansky et al. typology, neglectful parents exhibit the following traits:

- an inability to recognize or meet their children's needs
- an attempt to escape through alcohol, drugs, or sexual promiscuity
- frequent instances of single parent families
- possible history of deviant behavior
- isolation from the larger community and its resources
- a childlike demeanor
- a burden of physical and psychological ailments.

Frequently the neglectful parent's life represents a history of generations living in disorder, poverty, and neglect. These parents have not learned during their own childhood how to parent effectively. Perhaps they have never felt that anyone outside their own little network cares about them. In working with Mrs. Benner, for example, the social worker's task will be a difficult one. If the decision is made to let the children remain in the home, it will be necessary to communicate to the mother that someone does care; that her problems will not so totally overwhelm this helper that she will once again be left alone. Beyond the establishment of trust with a representative of the community, she can be put in touch with other community resources such as visiting nurses, financial aid, day care, fuel assistance, teaching of homemaker skills, which will greatly enhance her lifestyle. In other words, treatment of neglectful parents consists largely of "parenting the parents" so that they can learn to parent their children.

THE SEXUALLY ABUSIVE PARENT

Although parents teach their children to beware of strangers, it is not the stranger who presents the greatest danger. Seventy to 85 percent (depending upon the source) of sexual abusers are known to the child, and at least one half of that percentage may be a relative or family member.

If a child is molested by someone he or she does not know, it is vital that both the child and the family receive help to prevent the child from internalizing the trauma and the family from unconsciously perpetuating it by denial. The same is true if the child is molested by an acquaintance or more distant relative.

Who in fact is the perpetrator of a sexual abuse? Most abusers (97 percent) are male (10, p. 38). They are likely to choose either girls or boys according to their typology. Girls, however, are more frequent victims.

A. Nicholas Groth, well known for his work with sexual offenders, cites several characteristics that he has seen demonstrated by these offenders. Such an offender may—

- appear more submissive than assertive especially in relationships. He may see himself as a victim and not in control of his life.
- feel isolated; a loner who does not belong in relationship to others.
- feel fearful, depressed, and doubtful of his own worth, rejected by the outside world.
- not seem to be able to derive pleasure from or feel security in life—thus causing him to replace adults with a child who symbolizes his own immaturity. (18, pp. 229-30)

Groth explains further that the offender's insecurities appear as either aggression and dominance in his family or passivity and dependence. For example, Mr. Daniels and Mr. Walker, both members of the local PTA, were in direct contrast with each other.

Mr. Daniels, a long-time PTA president, was outspoken, aggressive, and highly verbal. He ruled his retiring wife and two daughters with a stern hand. For those who knew him, his aggressiveness better masked a profound sense of insecurity. It became obvious that beyond a superficial directing relationship with adults, he could not cope with any more equal liaison. His unrelenting overstrictness with his eldest teenage daughter was eventually brought to the attention of school officials, resulting in the final disclosure of their incestuous relationship.

Mr. Walker was the new husband of Thelma Walker, another assertive individual. He was as shy as his wife was outgoing, creating an interesting contrast. Through marriage he had inherited several young sons who were unlike their mother and as retiring as their new stepfather. It was not until several years after the marriage that school officials learned through other children that mild-mannered Mr. Walker was sexually abusing his eight-year-old stepson.

Groth divides sexual offenders into two categories: fixated and regressed. Those in the fixated category exhibit the following characteristics:

- an interest in children that started during adolescence
- main interest in children as opposed to adults
- more likely to molest boys
- great difficulty in relating to peers
- overwhelmed by the logistics of life
- sexually victimized as children (true of about 50 percent of offenders) at about the same age as their child victims
- relationships with women usually initiated by women
- chaotic childhood with numerous moves, illnesses, or parental marriage problems
- frequently seem like children to their wives
- show little or no guilt for the sexual abuse. (35, pp. 99-104)

The fixated abuser usually chooses boys because he sees' himself in them and mentally lowers himself to their level. He perceives himself at the same maturity level as his victim and therefore a peer. Although this offender may also choose a girl victim, he views her in much the same way. In short, he tries to join with his victim, seeking the undemanding love he feels he did not receive as a child.

The regressed offender may have developed normally as far as sexual preference is concerned, but has found adult relationships and lifestyle beyond his ability to cope. Most often this offender is married, has done fairly well with peers to this point, and has carried out his role as an adult adequately. His present life may be wrought with stress such as unemployment, marital problems, moves, crises, sudden sexual dysfunction, new disability (retirement or aging). Unlike the fixated offender, he does not necessarily premeditate the relationship. It is more a case of something that "just happened" in his mind. Thus there is a scenario of a man who—

- has a primary interest in agemates.
- has a recently developed interest in children.
- may have begun abusing impulsively.
- is under a lot of stress.
- continues to have sexual experiences with adults as well as with children.
- may be more likely to be involved with alcohol.
- is attracted to girl victims.
- is usually married. (35, pp. 104-9)

The regressed abuser chooses children because they offer a nonconflictual, undemanding relationship of warm, mutual dependence and love. He elevates the child to his age level, seeing her as more mature and womanly. He too is seeking the all-loving relationship that will give him a feeling of importance.

What part does this abuser play in the child's life? He may be a relative, a friend of the family, a neighbor, a babysitter, or even a father. (Some cases of mother-son or mother-daughter incest have been reported, but usually the incestuous parent is the father.) Blair and Rita Justice discuss the incestuous father (somewhat overlapping Groth's ideas on characteristics of the abuser) in *The Broken Taboo: Sex in the Family* (23). Along with the introvert and the tyrant, they mention another motivational type called the rationalizer. This individual rationalizes that his incestuous involvement with his daughter is based upon his desire to teach her about sex, his deep love for her, his desire to protect her from others who may use her for sexual purposes; or in some cases the father believes in total sexual freedom in the home (23, pp. 62-80).

Whatever the typology of the father, how does the mother fit into this complex domestic puzzle? Why would she "stand by" allowing her daughter to be abused? Some theorists feel that on some level—either conscious or unconscious—the mother knows about the relationship or at least suspects and cannot bring herself to admit her fears. This mother usually—

- depends financially or emotionally upon her husband.
- participates in role reversal with her daughter so that the girl has taken much of the responsibility from the mother.
- satisfies the basic needs of her children, but may not be participating in nurturing.
- is seen by her daughter as having failed the father.
- has a strained and unsuccessful relationship with her daughter.
- is absent at prime nurturing hours such as bedtime. (Her absence may take the form of illness, working long hours or late, or being involved in activities outside the home.)
- has a poor self-image.
- fails to set limits in her home.
- has unreasonable expectations of her husband and children (may expect them to nurture her).
- may have been abused as a child herself.
- may not be interested or enjoyably involved in a sexual relationship with her husband. (35, pp. 172-81; 37, pp. 195-202)

Like her husband, the mother may be either dominant or dependent. In rare cases, when it is the mother who is the abuser and the father who stands aside, the characteristics of abuser and spouse are similar. The mother, too overwhelmed by life's stresses, sees her child (usually a son) as someone to whom she can turn for nurture.

Whether the molester is father or mother, incestuous families can usually be identified by similar characteristics. Such families demonstrate—

- an oversecretiveness in almost all their activities
- an overly possessive or restrictive attitude toward the daughter (especially on the father's part in father-daughter incest)
- blurred generational boundaries (generations do not have clear-cut roles—parents and children seem more like peers in their behavior)
- an atmosphere where siblings show marked jealousy toward one child who seems favored
- frequent opportunities for father and daughter to be alone.

Incestuous families guard their "secret" at all costs, often going to great lengths to preserve it.

There is another type of abuser whom some sources place in a separate category—the adolescent abuser. Adolescents are presented with numerous opportunities to molest children. Their role as babysitter is one prime chance. This is not to say that the number of trustworthy teenage babysitters does not far outweigh the potential abusers, but the opportunity exists for the latter nevertheless. Teenage boys are at the height of their sexual curiosity. Some may be experiencing too much conflict in their activities and may turn to children as a less demanding alternative.

A telling sign of a teenage boy who might be tempted to exploit children is a lack of contact with his peers. If the boy's willingness to help us with small children isn't *balanced* with an interest in peer activities and relationships, there might be reason to be concerned. (35, p.91)

Older siblings may also be in a position to abuse much younger brothers and sisters.

The question often arises: "What is the difference between sexual exploration between agemates—considered a normal sideline of sexual awakening—and the sexual abuse of one minor by another?" One of the best rules of thumb relates to the level of power, knowledge, and resources each person has attained. In addition, most theorists agree that five years difference between the age of the older and the younger child in sexual interaction is usually the crucial difference (35, p. 90).

Whatever the particular symptoms the sexual abuser exhibits, the fact remains that the child suffers. An understanding of the behavior should, it is hoped, help teachers in their attempts to help the child.

THE EMOTIONALLY ABUSIVE PARENT

The parent who emotionally abuses a child may have some of the same characteristics as the physically abusive or even the neglectful parent. The most obvious trait shared by all these individuals is an extremely poor self-image that manifests itself by striking out verbally as well as physically against someone closest to them—in this case, the child. Even more obviously than the other types of abusers, emotionally abusive parents come from all socioeconomic levels. Frequently, however, they too have been victims of childhoods that have prevented them from growing emotionally. Their family experiences—from life with a skid-row alcoholic to life with a wealthy public figure—may have been as different as their personalities.

Emotionally abusive parents include not only those who belittle, criticize, or even torture the child, but also those who fail to provide the support or affection that promote the child's healthy development. The latter condition is sometimes referred to as emotional neglect. Parents who have had little physical touching, affection, or encouragement from their own parents may have been deprived of a great deal of the emotional satisfaction that young children need. As a result of their own childhood experiences, they may neglect very vital needs of their own offspring—by not wanting the child, by being afraid of spoiling the child, by being reluctant to touch the child, or by not having time for the child.

In other words, emotionally neglectful parents may not comprehend the importance of reassurance, encouragement, and endearments to their offspring. If they do not feel comfortable about their own strengths and accomplishments, it will be difficult for them to recognize and acknowledge those of their child.

Emotionally abusive parents who are aggressive rather than neglectful in their acts are more difficult to understand, but perhaps they are more in need of understanding. These are individuals whose lives have taught them not to expect success, affection, and attention. Often they have a bitter attitude toward the hidden disappointments of the past. They may see the child as an extension of themselves with the deficiencies painfully obvious. Or the child may be a symbol of a hated spouse, a parent perceived to be unfair or cruel, or an unfulfilled dream. Frequently, because of their own problems, these parents have little ability to realize the profound effect their criticisms, threats, or tortures may be having on the child. Therapy to improve their view of self may be the only way to help the child.

Whether the abuse or neglect is physical, emotional, or sexual, abusive and neglectful parents need help. They live in a world filled with pain and frustrations with which they have never learned to cope. The first step in helping such parents—and their children—is to see that their problems come to the attention of someone who can help.

Chapter 8

How Can You Help the Child by Helping the Family?

UNDERSTANDING THE PARENTS

Understanding the pathology involved in the abuse and neglect of children may on the one hand be helpful. On the other hand, no matter how great the intellectual understanding, when it comes to working with an abusive or neglectful parent, it may not be very easy to be the all-forgiving, all-knowing person one would wish to be. When a child has been hurt, concern for the child makes it difficult to forgive the adult who should have been capable of enough control or wisdom to protect the child. In the past abusive parents were imprisoned for their misdeeds. History teaches, however, that one of the most effective ways to help the child is to understand and help the parent. An experienced high school teacher admitted the following reaction:

When I learned that Peggy was pregnant by her own father I was horrified. It was so against what I valued and believed in, I wondered what kind of monster could do this. When I first had to meet with Mr. C. I felt really ill. I conjured up retaliatory measures such as imprisonment for life or even castration. And yet when I finally met him I was stunned to realize who he was. Tom C.—that shy, unpopular boy I had attended high school with years before. I remembered the paintings he had done during art class—the pleading for understanding in his every look and brush stroke. After I was able to think of the misunderstood person beneath the outward appearance, I realized how I had looked at so many abusive and neglectful parents. Blinded by what they were doing to *my* students, I had not given myself a chance to realize that they were so thoroughly out of control of themselves and their lives they were but children themselves.

Of course not all teachers have the advantage of knowing abusive parents before they come to the attention of society in such a despicable way. Nevertheless, it would be fairly safe to say that the problems of most of these parents are related to feelings of isolation that had their roots much earlier in their lives. Although their actions certainly cannot be condoned, the condemnation of society's intervention sends a message.

Building their lives back to the point of being able to adequately care for their children—if this construction is possible—is a huge task, and to do this they need many helpers.

HELPING THE PARENTS

Although it is the role of the social service agency to treat the parents, the child's teacher can also be of great help. The suggestions that follow discuss some ways that teachers can aid parents—and indirectly the child.

1. *Approach the parents in a noncondemnatory manner, no matter how you may be feeling.* Indicating that you know how difficult it is for them to be in this situation may create a feeling that you are an ally. Try to assure the parents that you know that they love their child and want to do their best for the child in the future. Despite the apparent message of their actions, this is more than likely true.

2. *Keep the parents up-to-date on the child's progress.* Parents need to feel in control. They need to think that you and they are intent upon the same thing: the child's best interest. You may have to reach out to them and overlook, in your own mind, the frustration of initial rejection. If this rejection continues, all you can do is figuratively leave the door open for future communication.

3. *Encourage parental involvement in school programs and activities—PTA, adult education, parenting programs, other parent groups.* Remember that these parents have been isolated with little or no support and they need contact with peers. Some may not receive your suggestions with enthusiasm, but after your careful coaxing, sending meeting announcements home with the child, asking other parents to reach out, they may eventually respond. Other parents may welcome this new attention readily.

Adult education programs not only provide socialization, but they also teach skills that the abusive parent can use as an outlet. One abusive mother, for example, enrolled in a ''Know Your Auto'' course designed primarily to familiarize participants with the workings of a car either to make minor repairs or to recognize possible trouble when consulting a mechanic. As a single parent, one of this woman's most stressful experiences centered around transportation and an aging car. Knowing her car helped her to feel more in control and thus freed her from one more stress.

In one school, a colleague and I led a *parent support group* created and sponsored by the school to assist parents in dealing with the everyday issues of parenting. Such an activity can be extremely helpful to the insecure parent. This group discussed ways to handle specific situations, invited speakers on a variety of child management topics, and generally provided support for participants in parenting endeavors. One of the more

74

successful programs in dealing with abusive parents is Parents Anonymous, a support group specifically for such parents. (See Appendix D.)

Parenting skills workshops are another method to strengthen parental confidence. Parent Awareness, for example, is a group learning experience designed to help parents explore positive alternatives in parenting. A series of workshops examines such important topics as explaining sexuality to children, positive methods of discipline, handling sibling issues, building a positive self-image and independence, dealing with children's fears, understanding child development, explaining death to a child, helping children adjust to divorce, and dealing with feelings in general. A comprehensive program such as this is worthwhile for all parents, but it is especially helpful to those who have difficulty coping. (See Appendix H.)

Courses in child development are useful too. The fact that some parents have too high expectations for their children points out the importance of such courses. Knowledge of child development should encourage more realistic parental expectations for children of various ages.

Other professionals within the school setting can also be helpful. Nurses can conduct health-related workshops or enlighten parents as to the types of testing available. Guidance personnel or others schooled in career development can provide counseling or workshops on job skill inventories. The list continues, stressing as much enhancement of parental potential as possible.

4. *Above all, try to discern parental strengths and focus on them.* Encourage parents in areas where you know they will meet with success. As a social worker, I used to try to discover at least one or two strengths whenever I met with abusive or neglectful clients. It was not always easy, but I found that it helped me to help them engineer their own successes.

Certainly teachers' conference time is limited. It is possible, however, to carry on excellent relationships with parents through notes. A friendly note praising a child's latest accomplishment, especially if taught by the parent, is enough to brighten the day of an otherwise isolated, overwrought caretaker.

5. *Know how your community can help.* If you do not know how to help the parents, consider finding out about local referral sources. For example, many communities have crisis hotlines for parents who cannot cope. (The local protective service agency or United Way or community services organization may have such a list.) Keep these telephone numbers available to give to the distraught parent.

Most of all, in working with abusive and neglectful parents, creativity is vital. Social services have not discovered all the answers in treatment. It could well be the support or a program offered by the local school system or its staff that makes the difference for the troubled parent, and thus for the maltreated child.

Chapter 9

What Can You Do About Prevention?

Throughout, this book has alluded to the concept of prevention in a variety of ways. However, prevention cannot be stressed emphatically enough and at the very least deserves a separate chapter.

IMMEDIATE MEASURES

Proportionate to the increase in community awareness over the last few years is the number of programs geared to educating both children and adults about child abuse and neglect. Many of these are excellent. Some are aimed at specifics such as Elaine Krause's filmstrips for children on sexual abuse. Others, such as the Personal Safety Curriculum, although geared to sexual abuse, consider a variety of childhood concerns as well. (See Appendix H.)

Whether you show a film or filmstrip, use a previously designed program, or discuss the subject in your classroom, children should be made aware of the types of abuse and neglect, and should have some idea of what to do if they or any of their friends are victims. In recent years the concept of children's rights has been defined and redefined by a multitude of concerned groups and individuals. Teachers can prevent or at least inspire the reporting of abuse and neglect by helping children become aware of their rights. These include the meeting of basic human needs—for food, shelter, safety, and affection.

One creative teacher asked the children to cut out a multicolored pyramid (resembling Maslow's hierarchy of needs included in many psychology or organizational behavior texts) and to label each segment according to the level of needs represented. For example, at the bottom was the need to be physically comfortable. The children learned that if they were physically uncomfortable for some reason (hunger or fatigue, for example), they had trouble doing less tangible things such as learning or creating.

As they begin to understand their own needs, children can realize when these are not being met consistently and they may perhaps be able to ask for help.

Youngsters also have the right to learn about and to be protected from physical abuse. Many sexual abuse programs stress two additional rights for children—the right to privacy and the right to their own bodies, encompassing the right to be touched only when and how they choose.

Another part of personal safety programs helps children realize that it may sometimes be appropriate to say no to adults, especially in cases of attempted sexual abuse. At this point it is important to distinguish between rights and responsibilities. Each person has the responsibility to try to become a healthy, capable adult, and adults have the responsibility to see that children develop in this way. Therefore saying no to a request to perform a reasonable chore such as cleaning up one's room is of course inappropriate. On the other hand, saying no to an activity that is harmful to the child, such as physical or sexual abuse, is a right, because the harmful act is detrimental to the development and training to become an effective and responsible adult. Obviously, it is important to discuss rights as a prevention tool sensitively, with the overall message that most concerned adults want to help children protect their rights.

A prerequisite of protecting one's own rights is the feeling that one is worthwhile and therefore important enough to *have* rights. Chapter 6 discusses the need to enhance the child's self-image. Self-confident children do not usuallly become victims. Classroom exercises that help children value themselves may also serve to prevent future victimization.

Part of any prevention program is the identification of those adults to whom children can turn in crises. In case of a fire, they would call the fire department or in case of a crime, the police. Children should also be helped to think about whom to call or approach in a variety of other crises. The film *Who Do You Tell?* (see Appendix H) puts children through such an exercise. The child who knows when to say no and to whom to turn in trouble is the child best armed to prevent or stop abuse.

LONG-TERM MEASURES

Thus far the discussion has emphasized prevention in the immediate or impending sense; it has not looked at the long-range aspects. It is in fact possible to arm children so that they themselves may not become abusers in the future. According to experts, contemporary society is violent, laden with sexual innuendos and compulsions toward self-gratification—a stage set with the necessary props for future maltreatment of children. There are, however, several areas of positive influence that educators can exert within the classroom to prevent such harm.

One way to start is with the tasks that abusive parents have not learned. (See Chapter 7.) Little lessons in how to make decisions, how to delay gratification, how to express one's needs, how to take responsibility for one's own actions, and how to tell the difference between feelings and actions can help create a more mature adult who does not fit the profile of an abuser. Teaching children to solve problems can also equip them with skills to prevent their becoming overwhelmed by stresses. Abusive parents are frequently so overcome by little problems that they are at a loss to know how to cope until these problems seem resistant to solution.

Adults in the working world use many catch phrases such as stress management or stress reduction, but few think to teach their children how to recognize and handle stress in their young lives. The little stresses of childhood are as important to the child as impending mergers to the corporate executive. And as the child grows, they have a way of blossoming into adult-level stresses. Why not teach youngsters to recognize what is stressful to them, handle it efficiently, and possibly not be overwhelmed in adulthood? For younger children, such material can be presented in the form of a game. For example, have children brainstorm a problem and solutions, and then offer the problem holder the right to decide how to handle it.

In addition, child management information is important knowledge for many youngsters to possess. Abusive parents are often ill-informed about child development. Teachers may therefore want to institute child development/management classes or segments of parenting courses. Even small children would enjoy a visit from a baby or younger child combined with a discussion of the child's needs and behavior at a particular age. I personally believe that every high school should offer a class on parenting skills.

Perhaps, the best tool to give children in this complex, impersonal society is the ability to build a functioning support system. Abusive parents are often devoid of such emotional inspiration and feel alone and isolated. Similar to the *Who Do You tell?* exercise, asking children whom they would approach in each emotional crisis helps them realize the importance of friends and family.

However they accomplish the task, classroom teachers have many opportunities—if not a duty—to educate children in the prevention of abuse and neglect. After all, prevention is hope for the future.

BIBLIOGRAPHY

1. Allen, Charlotte Vale. *Daddy's Girl.* New York: Wyndham Books, 1981

2. Brady, Katherine. *Father's Days: A True Story of Incest.* New York: Seaview Books, 1979.

3. Burgess, Ann Wolbert; Groth, A. Nicholas; Halstrom, Lynda Lytle; and Sgroi, Suzanne M. *Sexual Assault of Children and Adolescents.* Lexington, Mass.: Lexington Books, 1978.

4. Castillo, Gloria A. *Left-Handed Teaching: Lessons in Affective Education.* New York: Praeger Publishing, 1974.

5. Caulfield, Barbara. *The Legal Aspects of Protective Services for Abused and Neglected Children.* Washington, D.C.: U.S. Department of Health, Education and Welfare, 1978.

6. Chalmers, Mary Jane. "The Murder of Robbie Wayne, Age Six." *Reader's Digest,* November 1980.

7. Christiansen, James. *Educational and Psychological Problems of Abused Children.* Saratoga, Calif.: Century 21 Publishing Co., 1980.

8. Collins, Marva, and Tamarkin, Civia. *Marva Collins' Way.* Los Angeles: J. P. Tarcher, 1982.

9. Davis, James R. *Help Me, I'm Hurt: The Child Abuse Handbook.* Dubuque, Iowa: Kendall/Hunt Publishing Co., 1982.

10. DeFrancis, Vincent. *Protecting the Child Victim of Sex Crimes Committed by Adults: Final Report.* Denver, Colo.: American Humane Association, 1968.

11. Denker, Henry. *The Scofield Diagnosis.* New York: Simon and Schuster, 1977.

12. Finkelhor, David. "What's Wrong with Sex Between Children and Adults?" *American Journal of Orthopsychiatry* 49, no. 4 (October 1979): 692-97.

13. _____. *Sexually Victimized Children.* New York: Free Press, 1979.

14. Fisher, B.; Berdie, J.; Cook, J.; and Day, N. *Adolescent Abuse and Neglect: Intervention Strategies.* Washington, D.C.: U.S. Department of Health and Human Services, 1980.

15. Fontana, Vincent J. *Somewhere a Child Is Crying: Maltreatment—Causes and Prevention.* New York: Mentor Books, New American Library, 1973.

16. Giovannoni, Jeanne M., and Becerra, Rosina M. *Defining Child Abuse.* New York: Free Press, 1979.

17. Goldstein, Joseph; Freud, Anna; and Solnit, Albert J. *Beyond the Best Interests of the Child.* New York: Free Press, 1973.

18. Groth, A. Nicholas. "The Incest Offender." In *Handbook of Clinical Intervention in Child Sexual Abuse,* edited by Suzanne Sgroi. Lexington, Mass.: Lexington Books, 1982.

19. Hally, Carolyn; Polansky, Nancy F.; Polansky, Norman A. *Child Neglect Mobilizing Services.* Washington, D.C.: U.S. Department of Health and Human Services, 1980.

20. Helfer, Ray E. *Childhood Comes First: A Crash Course in Childhood for Adults.* East Lansing, Mich.: Ray E. Helfer, 1978.

21. _____, and Kempe, C. Henry. *Child Abuse: The Family and the Community.* Cambridge, Mass.: Ballinger Publishing Co., 1976.

22. Howe, Leland W., and Howe, Mary Martha. *Personalizing Education: Values Clarification and Beyond.* New York: Hart Publishing Co., 1975.

23. Justice, Blair, and Justice, Rita. *The Broken Taboo: Sex in the Family.* New York: Human Sciences Press, 1979.

24. Justice, Rita, and Justice, Blair. *The Abusing Family.* New York: Human Sciences Press, 1976.

25. Katz, Sanford N. *When Parents Fail: The Law's Response to Family Breakdown.* Boston, Mass.: Beacon Press, 1971.

26. Kempe, C. Henry, and Helfer, Ray E. *Helping the Battered Child and His Family.* New York: J. B. Lippincott Co., 1972.

27. Knight, Michael E. *Teaching Children to Love Themselves.* Englewood Cliffs, N.J.: Prentice-Hall, 1982.

28. Landau, Hortense R.; Salus, Marsha K.; Stiffarm, Thelma; with Kalb, Nora Lee. *Child Protection: The Role of the Courts.* Washington, D.C.: U.S. Department of Health and Human Services, 1980.

29. Leavitt, Jerome E. *The Battered Child: Selected Readings.* Fresno, Calif.: California State University, 1974.

30. Martin, Harold P. *Treatment for Abused and Neglected Children.* Washington, D.C.: U.S. Department of Health, Education and Welfare, 1979.

31. Meiselman, Karin C. *Incest.* San Francisco, Calif.: Jossey-Bass, 1978.

32. Niatove, Connie. "Arts Therapy with Sexually Abused Children." In *Handbook of Clinical Intervention in Child Sexual Abuse,* edited by Suzanne Sgroi. Lexington, Mass.: Lexington Books, 1982.

33. Polansky, Norman A.; Chalmers, Mary Ann; Buttenweiser, Elizabeth; and Williams, David P. *Damaged Parents: An Anatomy of Child Neglect.* Chicago: University of Chicago Press, 1981.

34. Ragan, Cynthia.; Salus, Marsha K.; and Schutze, Gretchen. *Child Protection: Providing Ongoing Services.* Washington, D.C.; U.S. Department of Health and Human Services, 1980.

35. Sanford, Linda Tschinhart. *The Silent Children: A Parent's Guide to the Prevention of Child Sexual Abuse.* Garden City, N.Y.: Anchor Press/Doubleday, 1980.

36. *Sexual Abuse of Children: Selected Readings.* Washington, D.C.: U.S. Department of Health and Human Services, 1980 (#78-30161).

37. Sgroi, Suzanne, ed. *Handbook of Clinical Intervention in Child Sexual Abuse.* Lexington, Mass.: Lexington Books, 1982.

38. Stember, Clara Jo. "Art Therapy: A New Use in the Diagnosis and Treatment of Sexually Abused Children." In *Sexual Abuse of Children: Selected Readings.* Washington, D.C.: U.S. Department of Health and Human Services, 1980 (#78-30161).

39. Walters, David R. *Physical and Sexual. Abuse of Children: Causes and Treatment.* Bloomington, Ind.: Indiana University Press, 1975.

40. Wells, Harold C., and Canfield, Jack. *One Hundred Ways to Enhance Self-Concepts in the Classroom: Handbook for Teachers and Parents.* New York: Prentice-Hall, 1976.

41. Young, Leontine, *Wednesday's Children: A Study of Child Neglect and Abuse.* New York: McGraw-Hill Book Co., 1964.

APPENDICES

APPENDIX A

PHYSICAL AND BEHAVIORAL INDICATOR

Type of Child Abuse/Neglect	Physical Indicators	Behavioral Indicators
PHYSICAL ABUSE	Unexplained bruises and welts: —on face, lips, mouth —on torso, back, buttocks, thighs —in various stages of healing —clustered, forming regular patterns —reflecting shape of article used to inflict (electric cord, belt buckle) —on several different surface areas —regularly appear after absence, weekend, or vacation --human bite marks —bald spots Unexplained burns: —cigar, cigarette burns, especially on soles, palms, back, or buttocks —immersion burns (sock-like, glove-like, doughnut-shaped on buttocks or genitalia) —patterned like electric burner, iron, etc. —rope burns on arms, legs, neck, or torso Unexplained fractures: —to skull, nose, facial structure —in various stages of healing —multiple or spiral fractures Unexplained lacerations or abrasions: —to mouth, lips, gums, eyes —to external genitalia	Wary of adult contacts Apprehensive when other children c Behavioral extremes: —aggressiveness, or —withdrawal —overly compliant Afraid to go home Reports injury by parents Exhibits anxiety about normal activities, e.g., napping Complains of soreness and moves awkwardly Destructive to self and others Early to school or stays late as if afraid to go home Accident prone Wears clothing that covers body when not appropriate Chronic runaway (especially adolescents) Cannot tolerate physical contact: or touch
PHYSICAL NEGLECT	Consistent hunger, poor hygiene, inappropriate dress Consistent lack of supervision, especially in dangerous activities or long periods Unattended physical problems or medical needs Abandonment Lice Distended stomach, emaciated	Begging, stealing food Constant fatigue, listlessness or falling asleep States there is no caretaker at home Frequent school absence or tardine Destructive, pugnacious School dropout (adolescents) Early emancipation from family (adolescents)

pe of Child use/Neglect	Physical Indicators	Behavioral Indicators
EXUAL BUSE	Difficulty in walking or sitting Torn, stained or bloody underclothing Pain or itching in genital area Bruises or bleeding in external genitalia, vaginal or anal areas Venereal disease Frequent urinary or yeast infections Frequent unexplained sore throats	Unwilling to participate in certain physical activities Sudden drop in school performance Withdrawal, fantasy or unusually infantile behavior Crying with no provocation Bizarre, sophisticated, or unusual Anorexia (especially adolescents) sexual behavior or knowledge Sexually provocative Poor peer relationships Reports sexual assault by caretaker Fear of or seductiveness toward males Suicide attempts (especially adolescents) Chronic runaway Early pregnancies
MOTIONAL 1ALTREAT- 1ENT	Speech disorders Lags in physical development Failure to thrive (especially in infants) Asthma, severe allergies, or ulcers Substance abuse	Habit disorders (sucking, biting, rocking, etc.) Conduct disorders (antisocial, destructive, etc.) Neurotic traits (sleep disorders, inhibition of play) Behavioral extremes: —compliant, passive —aggressive, demanding Overly adaptive behavior: —inappropriately adult —inappropriately infantile Developmental lags (mental, emotional) Delinquent behavior (especially adolescents)

Adapted from Broadhurst, D. D..; Edmunds, M.: MacDicken, R.A. *Early Childhood Programs and the Prevention and Treatment of Child Abuse and Neglect.* The User Manual Series. Washington, D.C.: U.S. Department of Health, Education and Welfare, 1979.

APPENDIX B

WHO MUST REPORT

States and Territories	"Any Person" or "Any Other Person"**	Physician	Nurse	Surgeon	Osteopath	Dentist	Resident	Intern	Hospital/Institution Personnel	Practitioner of Healing Arts	Chiropractor	Optometrist	Podiatrist	Pharmacist	Mental Health Professional	Coroner/Medical
Alabama		X	X	X	X	X			X		X	X	X	X	X	X
Alaska		X	X	X	X	X			X	X	X	X			X	
Arizona		X	X	X	X	X	X	X			X		X		X	X
Arkansas		X	X	X	X	X	X	X	X						X	X
California		X	X	X		X	X	X	X		X		X			
Colorado		X	X	X	X	X		X	X		X		X		X	
Connecticut	X	X	X	X	X	X	X	X			X	X	X		X	
Delaware	X	X	X			X	X	X	X						X	
District of Columbia		X	X			X					X				X	X
Florida	X	X	X													
Georgia		X	X		X	X	X	X					X		X	•
Hawaii		X	X		X	X				X						
Idaho	X	X	X				X	X								
Illinois		X	X	X	X	X			X		X		X			
Indiana	X															
Iowa		X	X	X	X	X	X	X	X		X	X	X		X	
Kansas			X			X	X	X			X				X	
Kentucky	X	X	X		X	X	X	X	X		X	X			X	
Louisiana	X	X	X				X	X	X							
Maine		X	X		X	X	X	X			X		X		X	X
Maryland		X	X	X		X	X		X						X	
Massachusetts		X	X			X		X								
Michigan		X	X			X										X
Minnesota									X	X					X	
Mississippi		X	X			X	X	X							X	
Missouri		X	X			X	X	X	X	X	X	X	X		X	X
Montana	X	X	X													
Nebraska	X	X	X						X							
Nevada		X	X	X	X	X	X	X	X		X	X			X	
New Hampshire	X	X	X	X	X	X	X	X	X		X	X			X	
New Jersey	X															
New Mexico	X	X	X				X	X								
New York		X	X	X	X	X	X	X	X		X	X	X		X	
North Carolina		X	X	X	X	X	X	X	X		X	X	X		X	
North Dakota		X	X			X							X		X	X
Ohio		X	X	X		X	X	X					X		X	
Oklahoma	X	X	X	X	X	X	X	X								
Oregon		X	X			X	X	X			X	X			X	
Pennsylvania		X	X		X	X			X	X	X	X	X		X	
Rhode Island	X															
South Carolina		X	X			X					X		X		X	X
South Dakota		X	X	X	X	X	X	X			X	X	X		X	
Tennessee	X															
Texas	X															
Utah	X		X													
Vermont		X	X	X	X	X	X	X	X		X				•	
Virginia			X				X	X		X					X	
Washington		X	X	X	X	X					X	X	X	X	X	
West Virginia						X									X	
Wisconsin		X	X	X		X			X		X	X			X	
Wyoming	X															
America Samoa		X	X	X	X	X	X	X	X		X	X	X		X	
Guam		X	X	X	X	X		X	X	X	X	X	X		X	
Puerto Rico	X	X	X			X	X	X	X	X	X			X		
Virgin Islands		X	X			X			X						X	

*Adapted from *Child Abuse and Neglect State Reporting Laws.* Washington, D.C.: NCCAN, Children's Bureau, 1979.

**A state that does not specify categories of professionals that must report, but instead requires that every person or any person report, is checked only in this column.

WHO REPORTS

Teachers	Other School Personnel	Social Services Worker	Law Enforcement Officer	Peace Officer	Police Officers	Probation Officer	Parole Officer	Religious Healing Practitioner	Child Care Institution/Worker	Clergyman	Attorney	Others	States and Territories	Permissive Reporting
			WHO MUST REPORT										WHO MAY REPORT	
X	X	X	X	X					X			X	Alabama	•
X	†	X		X				X				X	Alaska	•
X	X	X		X								X	Arizona	
X	X	X	X	X					X				Arkansas	•
X	X	X		X		X		X	X	X		X	California	•
X	X	X							X	X		X	Colorado	•
X	X	X			X				X	X			Connecticut	
X	X	X											Delaware	
X	X	X	X						X				District of Columbia	•
X	†	X										X	Florida	
X	X	X	X						X				Georgia	•
X	†	X											Hawaii	•
X	†	X							X				Idaho	
X	X	X	X					X	X			X	Illinois	•
†	†												Indiana	
X	X	X		X					X				Iowa	•
X	X	X	X										Kansas	•
X	X	X		X					X			X	Kentucky	
X	†	X										X	Louisiana	•
X	X	X	X					X	X				Maine	•
X	X	X	X		X	X	X					X	Maryland	
X	X	X			X	X						X	Massachusetts	•
X	X	X	X						X			X	Michigan	•
X	X	X	X						X				Minnesota	•
X	X	X	X						X	X			Mississippi	
X	X	X	X	X		X	X	X	X	X		X	Missouri	•
X	†	X	X								X		Montana	
X	X	X											Nebraska	
X	X	X						X	X	X			Nevada	•
X	X	X	X					X	X	X		X	New Hampshire	
†	†												New Jersey	
X	†	X	X										New Mexico	
†·	X	X	X	X				X	X				New York	•
X	X	X	X					X				X	North Carolina	
X	X	X	X		X				X			X	North Dakota	•
X	X	X						X	X		X	X	Ohio	•
†	†												Oklahoma	
X	X	X		X					X	X	X	X	Oregon	
X	X	X	X	X				X	X			X	Pennsylvania	•
†·	†												Rhode Island	
X	X	X	X		X			X	X				South Carolina	•
X	X	X	X										South Dakota	•
†	†												Tennessee	
†	†												Texas	
†	†												Utah	
†	†				X							X	Vermont	•
X	X	X	X			X		X	X			X	Virginia	•
X	X	X						X	X			X	Washington	•
X	X	X	X	X				X	X			X	West Virginia	•
X	X	X	X		X				X				Wisconsin	•
†	†												Wyoming	
X	X	X	X	X				X	X				America Samoa	•
X	X	X	X	X				X	X			X	Guam	•
X	X	X							X				Puerto Rico	
X	X	X	X	X					X			X	Virgin Islands	•

†Teachers and other school personnel are required to report by state mandate of "any person" or "any other person" or "others."

APPENDIX C

WHERE CAN YOU FIND REPORTING INFORMATION?*

Since the responsibility for investigating reports of suspected child abuse and neglect lies at the state level, each state has established a child protective service reporting system. NCCAN annually compiles the descriptions of the reporting procedures in each state. Listed below are the names and addresses of the child protective services agency in each state, followed by the procedures for reporting suspected child maltreatment.

Alabama:
Alabama Department of Pensions and Security
64 North Union Street
Montgomery, Alabama 36130

Reports made to county 24-hour emergency telephone services.

Alaska:
Department of Health and Social Services
Division of Family and Youth Services
Pouch H-05
Juneau, Alaska 99881

Reports made to Division of Social Services field offices.

American Samoa:
Government of American Samoa
Office of the Attorney General
Pago Pago, American Samoa 96799

Reports made to the Department of Medical Services.

Arizona:
Department of Economic Security
P.O. Box 6123
Phoenix, Arizona 85005

Reports made to Department of Economic Security local offices.

Arkansas:
Arkansas Department of Human Services
Social Services Division
P.O. Box 1437
Little Rock, Arkansas 72203

Reports made to the statewide toll-free hotline (800) 482-5964.

California:
Department of Social Services
714-744 P Street
Sacramento, California 95814

Reports made to County Departments of Welfare and the Central Registry of Child Abuse (916) 445-7546 maintained by the Department of Justice.

Colorado:
Department of Social Services
1575 Sherman Street
Denver, Colorado 80203

Reports made to County Departments of Social Services.

---

*From "Everything You Always Wanted to Know About Child Abuse and Neglect and Asked!" Washington, D.C.: NCCAN (n.d.).

Connecticut:
Connecticut Department of Children
and Youth Services
Division of Children and Youth
Services
170 Sigourney Street
Hartford, Connecticut 06105

Reports made to (800) 842-2288.

Delaware:
Delaware Department of Health
and Social Services
Division of Social Services
P.O. Box 309
Wilmington, Delaware 19899

Reports made to statewide
toll-free reporting hotline
(800) 292-9582.

District of Columbia:
District of Columbia Department
of Human Services
Commission on Social Services
Family Services Administration
Child Protective Services
Division
First and I Streets, S.W.
Washington, D. C. 20024

Reports made to (202) 727-0995.

Florida:
Florida Department of Health
and Rehabilitative Services
1317 Winewood Boulevard
Tallahassee, Florida 32301

Reports made to (800) 342-9152

Georgia:
Georgia Department of Human
Resources
47 Trinity Avenue, S.W.
Atlanta, Georgia 30334

Reports made to County
Departments of Family and
Children Services.

Guam:
Child Welfare Services
Child Protective Services
P.O. Box 2816
Agana, Guam 96910

Reports made to the State Child
Protective Services Agency at
646-8417.

Hawaii:
Department of Social Services
and Housing
Public Welfare Division
Family and Children's Services
P.O. Box 339
Honolulu, Hawaii 96809

Reports made to the hotline
operated by Kapiolani-Children's
Medical Center on Oahu, and to
branch offices of the Division
on Hawaii, Maui, Kauai, Molakai.

Idaho:
Department of Health and Welfare
Child Protection
Division of Welfare
Statehouse
Boise, Idaho 83702

Reports made to Department of
Health and Welfare Regional Offices.

Illinois:
Illinois Department of Children and
Family Services
State Administrative Offices
One North Old State Capitol Plaza
Springfield, Illinois 62706

Reports made to (800) 25-ABUSE.

Indiana:
Indiana Department of Public Welfare
Division of Child Welfare -
Social Services
141 South Meridian Street, 6th Floor
Indianapolis, Indiana 46225

Reports made to County Departments
of Public Welfare.

Iowa:

Iowa Department of Human Services
Division of Community Programs
Hoover State Office Building
Fifth Floor
Des Moines, Iowa 50319

Reports made to the legally
mandated toll-free reporting
hotline (800) 362-2178

Kansas:

Kansas Department of Social and
Rehabilitation Services
Youth Services Division of
Children in Need of Care
Child Protection/Family
Services Section
Smith-Wilson Building
2700 West Sixth Street
Topeka, Kansas 66606

Reports made to Department of
Social and Rehabilitation
Services Area Offices.

Kentucky:

Kentucky Department for
Human Resources
275 East Main Street
Frankfort, Kentucky 40621

Reports made to County
Offices within 4 regions
of the state.

Louisiana:

Louisiana Department of Health
and Human Resources
Office of Human Development
Baton Rouge, Louisiana 70804

Reports made to the parish
protective service units.

Maine:

Maine Department of Human
Services
Human Services Building
Augusta, Maine 04333

Reports made to Regional Office
or to State Agency at
(800) 452-1999

Maryland:

Maryland Department of Human
Resources
Social Services Administration
300 W. Preston Street
Baltimore, Maryland 21201

Reports made to County
Departments of Social Services
or to local law enforcement
agencies.

Massachusetts:

Massachusetts Department of Social
Services
Protective Services
150 Causeway Street
Boston, Massachusetts 02114

Reports made to Regional Offices.

Michigan:

Michigan Department of Social
Services
300 S. Capitol Avenue
Lansing, Michigan 48926

Reports made to County
Departments of Social Welfare.

Minnesota:

Minnesota Department of Public
Welfare
Centennial Office Building
St. Paul, Minnesota 55155

Reports made to the County
Department of Public Welfare.

Mississippi:
  Mississippi Department of Public
    Welfare
  Division of Social Services
  P.O. Box 352
  Jackson, Mississippi 39216

  Reports made to (800) 222-8000.

Missouri:
  Missouri Department of Social
    Services
  Division of Family Services
  Broadway Building
  Jefferson City, Missouri 65101

  Reports made to (800) 392-3738.

Montana:
  Department of Social and
    Rehabilitation Services
  Social Services Bureau
  P.O. Box 4210
  Helena, Montana 59601

  Reports made to County Departments
  of Social and Rehabilitation
  Services.

Nebraska:
  Nebraska Department of
    Public Welfare
  301 Centennial Mall South
  5th Floor
  Lincoln, Nebraska 68509

  Reports made to local law
  enforcement agencies or to
  County Divisions of Public
  Welfare.

Nevada:
  Department of Human Resources
  Division of Welfare
  251 Jeanell Drive
  Carson City, Nevada 89710

  Reports made to Division of
  Welfare local offices.

New Hampshire:
  New Hampshire Department
    of Health and Welfare
  Division of Welfare
  Bureau of Child and Family
    Services
  Hazen Drive
  Concord, New Hampshire 03301

  Reports made to Division of
  Welfare District Offices.

New Jersey:
  New Jersey Division of Youth
    and Family Services
  P.O. Box 510
  One South Montgomery Street
  Trenton, New Jersey 08625

  Reports made to (800) 792-8610.
  District Offices also provide
  24-hour telephone service.

New Mexico:
  New Mexico Department of
    Human Services
  P.O. Box 2348
  Santa Fe, New Mexico 87503

  Reports made to County Social
  Service Offices or to
  (800) 432-6217.

New York:
  New York Department of
    Social Services
  Child Protective Services
  40 North Pearl Street
  Albany, New York 12207

  Reports made to (800) 342-3720
  or to District Offices.

North Carolina:
  North Carolina Department of Human
    Resources
  Division of Social Services
  325 North Salisbury Street
  Raleigh, North Carolina 27611

  Reports made to County Departments
  of Social Services.

North Dakota:
North Dakota Department of Human Services
Social Services Division
Children and Family Services Unit
Child Abuse and Neglect Program
Russel Building, Hwy. 83 North
Bismarck, North Dakota 58505

Reports made to Board of Social Services Area Offices and to 24-hour reporting services provided by Human Service Centers.

Ohio:
Ohio Department of Public Welfare
Bureau of Children Services
Children's Protective Services
30 E. Broad Street
Columbus, Ohio 43215

Reports made to County Departments of Public Welfare.

Oklahoma:
Oklahoma Department of Institutions, Social and Rehabilitative Services
Division of Social Services
P.O. Box 25352
Oklahoma City, Oklahoma 73125

Reports made to (800) 522-3511.

Oregon:
Department of Human Resources
Children's Services Division
Protective Services
509 Public Services Building
Salem, Oregon 97310

Reports made to local Children's Services Division Offices and to (503) 378-3016.

Pennsylvania:
Pennsylvania Department of Public Welfare
Office of Children, Youth and Families
Bureau of Family and Community Programs
1514 North 2nd Street
Harrisburg, Pennsylvania 17102

Reports made to the toll-free CHILDLINE (800) 932-0313.

Puerto Rico:
Puerto Rico Department of Social Services
Services to Families with Children
P.O. Box 11398
Fernandez Juncos Station
Santurce, Puerto Rico 00910

Reports made to local offices or to the Department.

Rhode Island:
Rhode Island Department for Children and Their Families
610 Mt. Pleasant Avenue
Providence, Rhode Island 02908

Reports made to State agency child protective services unit at (800) 662-5100 or to District Offices.

South Carolina:
South Carolina Department of Social Services
P.O. Box 1520
Columbia, South Carolina 29202

Reports made to County Departments of Social Services.

South Dakota:
  Department of Social Services
  Office of Children, Youth and
    Family Services
  Richard F. Kneip Building
  Pierre, South Dakota 57501

  Reports made to local offices.

Tennessee:
  Tennessee Department of Human
    Services
  State Office Building
  Room 410
  Nashville, Tennessee 37219

  Reports made to County Departments
  of Human Services.

Texas:
  Texas Department of Human Resources
  Protective Services for Children
    Branch
  P.O. Box 2960
  Austin, Texas 78701

  Reports made to (800) 252-5400.

Utah:
  Department of Social Services
  Division of Family Services
  150 West North Temple, Room 370
  P.O. Box 2500
  Salt Lake City, Utah 84103

  Reports made to Division of Family
  Services District Offices.

Vermont:
  Vermont Department of Social and
    Rehabilitative Services
  Social Services Division
  103 South Main Street
  Waterbury, Vermont 05676

  Reports made to State agency at
  (802) 828-3433 or to District
  Offices (24-hour services).

Virgin Islands:
  Virgin Islands Department of
    Social Welfare
  Division of Social Services
  P.O. Box 500
  Charlotte Amalie
  St. Thomas, Virgin Islands 00801

  Reports made to the Division of
  Social Services.

Virginia:
  Virginia Department of Welfare
  Bureau of Family and Community
    Programs
  Blair Building
  8007 Discovery Drive
  Richmond, Virginia 23288

  Reports made to (800) 552-7096
  in Virginia and (804) 281-9081
  outside the state.

Washington:
  Department of Social and Health
    Services
  Community Services Division
  Child Protective Services
  Mail Stop OB 41-D
  Olympia, Washington 98504

  Reports made to local Social
  and Health Services Offices.

West Virginia:
  Department of Welfare
  Division of Social Services
  Child Protective Services
  State Office Building
  1900 Washington Street E.
  Charleston, West Virginia 25305

  Reports made to (800) 352-6513.

Wisconsin:
  Wisconsin Department of Health
    and Social Services
  Division of Community Services
  1 West Wilson Street
  Madison, Wisconsin 53702

  Reports made to County Social
  Services Offices.

Wyoming:
  Department of Health and
    Social Services
  Division of Public Assistance and
    Social Services
  Hathaway Building
  Cheyenne, Wyoming 82002

  Reports made to County Departments
  of Public Assistance and Social
  Services.

APPENDIX D

WHERE CAN YOU FIND MORE INFORMATION?*

The address of the National Center on Child Abuse and Neglect is:

NCCAN
P.O. Box 1182
Washington, D.C. 20013

NCCAN also sponsors 10 regional resource centers. For more information, contact the regional center for your state:

Region I CAN Resource Center
Judge Baker Guidance Center
295 Longwood Avenue
Boston, MA 02115
Telephone: (617) 232-8390
(Connecticut, Maine, Massachusetts,
Rhode Island, Vermont, New Hampshire)

Region II CAN Resource Center
College of Human Ecology
Cornell University, MVR Hall
Ithaca, NY 14853
Telephone: (607) 256-7794
(New Jersey, New York, Puerto
Rico, Virgin Islands)

Region III CAN Resource Center
Howard University Institute for
   Urban Affairs and Research
2900 Van Ness Street, N.W.
Washington, D.C. 20008
Telephone: (202) 686-6770
(District of Columbia, Delaware,
Maryland, Pennsylvania, Virginia,
West Virginia)

Region IV CAN Southeastern Resource
   Center for Child and Youth Services
School of Social Work
University of Tennessee
Knoxville, TN 27996-3920
Telephone: (615) 974-6015
(Alabama, Florida, Georgia, Kentucky,
Mississippi, North Carolina, South
Carolina, Tennessee)

Region V CAN Resource Center
Graduate School of Social Work
University of Wisconsin-Milwaukee
Milwaukee, WI 53201
Telephone: (414) 963-4184
(Illinois, Indiana, Michigan,
Minnesota, Ohio, Wisconsin)

Region VI CAN Resource Center
Graduate School of Social Work
University of Texas at Austin
Austin, TX 78712
Telephone: (512) 471-4067
(Arkansas, Louisiana, New Mexico,
Oklahoma, Texas)

Region VII CAN Resource Center
Institute of Child Behavior
   and Development
University of Iowa-Oakdale Campus
Oakdale, IA 52319
Telephone: (319) 353-4791
(Iowa, Kansas, Missouri, Nebraska)

Region VIII CAN Resource Center
National Center for the Prevention &
   Treatment of Child Abuse and Neglect
1205 Oneida Street
Denver, CO 80220
Telephone: (303) 321-3963
(Colorado, Montana, North Dakota,
South Dakota, Utah, Wyoming)

*From "Everything You Always Wanted to Know About Child Abuse and Neglect and
Asked!" Washington, D.C.: NCCAN (n.d.).

Region IX CAN Resource Center
Department of Special Education
California State University
5151 State University Drive
Los Angeles, CA 90032
    Telephone: (213) 224-3283
(Arizona, California, Hawaii,
Nevada, Guam, Trust Territories)

Region X CAN Resource Center
Panel for Family Living
157 Yesler Way, #208
Seattle, WA 98104
    Telephone: (206) 624-1062
(Alaska, Idaho, Oregon, Washington)

Parents Anonymous, modeled after Alcoholics Anonymous, has chapters throughout the United States. For more information, or the location of the chapter in your community, contact:

> National Office of PA
> 22330 Hawthorne Boulevard
> Suite 208
> Torrance, California 90505
>
> Telephone: (213) 371-3501

Toll Free: (800) 421-0353   California only: (800) 352-0386

Parents United is a self-help organization for all family members affected by sexual abuse. For more information, contact:

> Parents United, Inc.
> P.O. Box 952
> San Jose, California 95102
>
> Telephone: (408) 280-5055

APPENDIX E

IMMUNITY*

States and Territories	Civil and Criminal Immunity in Making of a Report	Immunity for the Taking of Photographs	Immunity for the Taking of X-rays	Immunity in Resulting Judicial Proceedings	Requirement of Good Faith	Good Faith Presumed
Alabama	X			X		
Alaska	X			X	X	
Arizona	X			X	X	
Arkansas	X	X				X
California	X			X	X	
Colorado	X	X	X	X		X
Connecticut	X			X	X	
Delaware	X			X	X	
District of Columbia	X			X	X	X
Florida	X	X	X	X		X
Georgia	X			X	X	
Hawaii	X			X	X	
Idaho	X			X	X	
Illinois	X	X	X	X		X
Indiana	X	X	X	X	X	X
Iowa	X			X	X	
Kansas	X			X	X	
Kentucky	X			X		
Louisiana	X			X	X	
Maine	X			X		X
Maryland	X			X	X	
Massachusetts	X				X	
Michigan	X	X	X			X
Minnesota	X				X	
Mississippi	X			X		X
Missouri	X	X	X	X	X	
Montana	X			X		X
Nebraska	X			X	X	
Nevada	X			X	X	
New Hampshire	X			X	X	
New Jersey	X			X	X	
New Mexico	X			X		X
New York	X	X				X
North Carolina	X			X	X	
North Dakota	X				X	X
Ohio	X			X		
Oklahoma	X			X	X	
Oregon	X			X	X	
Pennsylvania	X	X		X	X	X
Rhode Island	X			X	X	
South Carolina	X			X	X	X
South Dakota	X			X	X	
Tennessee	X					X
Texas	X			X	X	
Utah	X	X	X		X	
Vermont	X			X	X	
Virginia	X			X	X	
Washington	X			X	X	
West Virginia	X	X	X		X	
Wisconsin	X	X			X	X
Wyoming	X	X	X		X	X
America Samoa	X	X			X	X
Guam	X	X		X	X	X
Puerto Rico	X					
Virgin Islands	X	X	X		X	

*From *Child Abuse and Neglect State Reporting Laws*. Washington, D.C.: NCCAN, Children's Bureau, 1979.

APPENDIX F

REPORTING PROCEDURE*

States and Territories	Orally, Followed By Writing	Time When Writing is Due	As Soon As Possible (ASAP) or Not Specified (NS)	Orally Only	Orally or In Writing	Orally, Then In Writing If Requested	Time When Due, If Requested	Procedure Not Specified	Receipt of Report Social Services Agency	Law Enforcement Agency	Other Agency
Alabama	X		NS						X	X	X
Alaska								X	X		
Arizona								X	X	X	
Arkansas						X	48 hours		X		
California	X	36 hours							X	X	X
Colorado	X		NS						X	X	
Connecticut	X	72 hours							X	X	
Delaware						X	NS		X		
District of Columbia						X	NS		X	X	
Florida	X		ASAP						X		
Georgia						X	NS		X		
Hawaii	X		ASAP						X		
Idaho								X		X	
Illinois	X	24 hours							X		
Indiana					X				X	X	
Iowa	X	48 hours							X		
Kansas						X	NS				X
Kentucky						X	48 hours		X		
Louisiana	X	5 days							X	X	
Maine						X	48 hours		X		
Maryland	X	48 hours							X	X	
Massachusetts	X	48 hours							X		
Michigan	X	72 hours							X		
Minnesota	X		ASAP						X	X	
Mississippi	X		ASAP						X		
Missouri	X	48 hours							X		
Montana								X	X		X
Nebraska	X		NS							X	
Nevada	X		ASAP						X	X	X
New Hampshire						X	48 hours		X		
New Jersey								X	X		
New Mexico								X	X		X
New York	X	48 hours							X		X
North Carolina					X				X		
North Dakota					X	X	48 hours		X		
Ohio						X	NS		X	X	X
Oklahoma	X		ASAP						X		
Oregon				X					X	X	
Pennsylvania	X	48 hours							X		
Rhode Island	X		NS						X		
South Carolina				X					X	X	
South Dakota				X					X		X
Tennessee								X	X	X	X
Texas	X	5 days							X	X	X
Utah						X	48 hours		X	X	
Vermont	X	7 days							X		
Virginia	X		NS						X		
Washington						X	NS		X	X	
West Virginia						X	48 hours		X		
Wisconsin						X	NS		X	X	
Wyoming						X	NS		X	X	
America Samoa						X	48 hours				X
Guam	X	48 hours							X		
Puerto Rico							48 hours		X		
Virgin Islands						X	48 hours				X

*From Child Abuse and Neglect State Reporting Laws. Washington, D.C.: NCCAN, Children's Bureau, 1979.

96

COMMONWEALTH OF MASSACHUSETTS – DEPARTMENT OF SOCIAL SERVICES

REPORT OF CHILD(REN) ALLEGED TO BE SUFFERING FROM SERIOUS PHYSICAL OR EMOTIONAL INJURY BY ABUSE OR NEGLECT*

Massachusetts law requires an individual who is a mandated reporter to **immediately** report any allegation of serious physical or emotional injury resulting from abuse or neglect to the Department of Social Services by oral communication. This written report must then be completed **within 48 hours** of making the oral report and should be sent to the appropriate Department office.

Please complete all sections of this form. If some data is unknown, please signify. If some data is uncertain, place a question mark after the entry.

DATA ON CHILDREN REPORTED:

	NAME	CURRENT LOCATION/ADDRESS	SEX	AGE OR DATE OF BIRTH
1)	Thomas Smythe, Jr.	195 East St., Westville, MA	☒ Male ☐ Female	10/09/72
2)			☐ Male ☐ Female	
3)			☐ Male ☐ Female	
4)			☐ Male ☐ Female	
5)			☐ Male ☐ Female	

DATA ON MALE GUARDIAN OR PARENT:

Name: Thomas   Brown
                   First   Last   Middle

Address: 195 East St.   Westville   MA
               Street and Number   City/Town   State

Telephone Number: 555-4567   Age: 40(?)

DATA ON FEMALE GUARDIAN OR PARENT:

Name: Gloria   Brown
                   First   Last   Middle

Address: 195 East St.   Westville   MA
               Street and Number   City/Town   State

Telephone Number: 555-4567   Age: 32

DATA ON REPORTER/REPORT:

     10/12/83   ☒ Mandatory Report   ☐ Voluntary Report
     Date of Report

Reporter's Name: Francine   Garcia   (teacher)
                      First   Last

Reporter's Address: (If the reporter represents an institution, school, or facility please indicate.)

South Westville Middle School   Westville
           Street   City/Town

     MA   555-3456
     State   Zip Code   Telephone Number

Has reporter informed caretaker of report?   ☐ YES   ☒ NO

ABUSE/NEGLECT REPORT - 3   (Revised April, 1983)

*Form reprinted with permission of Massachusetts Department of Social Services. *Filled-in data is fictitious and used only as an example.*

What is the nature and extent of the injury, abuse, maltreatment or neglect, including prior evidence of same? (Please cite the source of this information if not observed first hand.)

Tom has become increasingly withdrawn this school year. He apparently has no friends, eats alone, and has been seen crying on several occasions. In addition, the boy's grades are deteriorating and he is in danger of failing all subjects. According to other teachers, last year he did well in school and had many friends. Also, the school nurse reports that Tom appears to be losing weight.

What are the circumstances under which the reporter became aware of the injuries, abuse, maltreatment or neglect?

I called Tom's mother who reported that Mr. Brown has recently returned from a temporary assignment in Germany (he works for an oil company). The couple has been arguing about Mr. Brown's methods of discipline, which Mrs. Brown thinks are too harsh. They include isolating Tom from his half-brothers and sisters (Tom is from an earlier marriage of Mrs. Brown). For days at a time the boy is locked in his room from the time he gets home from school in the afternoon until he goes to school the next morning.

What action has been taken thus far to treat, shelter or otherwise assist the child to deal with this situation?

In my conversation with Tom's mother, she said there was nothing she could do. A parent/teacher conference was requested with both parents, but they refused this request. Tom was referred to the guidance counselor.

Please give other information which you think might be helpful in establishing the cause of the injury and/or the person responsible for it. If known, please provide the name(s) of the alleged perpetrator(s).

Tom told the guidance counselor that on some days the only meal he gets is lunch at school.

I would like to be contacted by the social worker.

Francine Garcia
Signature of Reporter

ABUSE/NEGLECT REPORT - 3   (Revised April, 1983)

APPENDIX H

SELECTED RESOURCES

Note: For easier identification the following key has been established:

S = Sexual abuse
N = Neglect
P = Physical abuse
M = Miscellaneous maltreatment

Further Reading for Educators

Bakan, David. *Slaughter of Innocents: A Story of the Battered Child Phenomenon.* San Francisco: Jossey-Bass, 1971. (M)

Brenton, M. "What Can Be Done About Child Abuse." *Today's Education* (September-October 1977): 30-33.

Broadhurst, D. D. "Policy-Making: First Step for Schools in the Fight Against Child Abuse and Neglect." *Elementary School Guidance and Counseling* 10 (1976): 222-26.

_____. "Update: What Schools Are Doing About Child Abuse and Neglect." *Children Today* (January-February 1978): 22-24.

Butler, Sandra. *Conspiracy of Silence: The Trauma of Incest.* San Francisco: New Glide Publications, 1978. (S)

Caskey, O.L., and Richardson, F. "Understanding and Helping Child Abuse Parents." *Elementary School Guidance and Counseling* 9 (1975): 196-208.

Chase, Naomi Feigelson. *A Child Is Being Beaten: Violence Against Children, An American Tragedy.* New York: Holt, Rinehart and Winston, 1975. (M)

Child Abuse and Neglect Project. *Education Policies and Practices Regarding Child Abuse and Neglect and Recommendations for Policy Development.* Denver: Education Commission of the States, 1976. (M)

_____. *Teacher Education: An Active Participant in Solving the Problem of Child Abuse and Neglect.* Denver: Education Commission of the States, 1977. (M)

Child Abuse and Neglect: The Problem of Its Management. Vols. 1, 2, and 3. Washington, D.C.: U.S. Department of Health, Education and Welfare, 1975. (M)

Child Sexual Abuse: Incest, Assault and Sexual Exploitation. Washington, D.C.: U.S. Department of Health and Human Services, 1981 (S)

Child Welfare League of America. *Standards for Child Protective Services.* New York: Child Welfare League of America, 1973. (M)

Children Alone: What Can Be Done About Abuse and Neglect. Reston, Va.: Council for Exceptional Children, 1977.

Davoren, E. "Foster Placement of Abused Children." *Children Today* 4, no. 2 (1975): 41. (P)

_____. "Working with Abusive Parents: A Social Worker's View." *Children Today* 4, no. 2 (1975): 38-43. (P)

DeFrancis, Vincent. *Protecting the Child Victim of Sex Crimes Committed by Adults*. Final Report. Denver: American Humane Association, Children's Division, 1969. (S)

Education Policies and Practices Regarding Child Abuse and Neglect and Recommendations for Policy Development. Denver: Education Commission of the States, 1976.

Finkelhor, David. *Sexually Victimized Children*. New York: Macmillan, 1979. (S)

Flomenhaft, K.; Machotka, Paul; Pittman, F. S. "Incest as a Family Affair" *Family Process* 6, no. 1: 98-116. (S)

Fontana, Vincent J. *Somewhere a Child Is Crying: Maltreatment, Causes and Prevention*. New York: Macmillan, 1973. (M)

Forward, S., and Buck, C. *Betrayal of Innocence: Incest and Its Devastation*. New York: Penguin Books, 1978. (S)

Fraser, Brian G. *The Educator and Child Abuse*. National Committee for Prevention of Child Abuse, Suite 510, 111 E. Wacker Dr., Chicago, IL 60601. (M)

Geiser, Robert, *Hidden Victims*. Boston: Beacon Press, 1979. (S)

Geiser, Robert L. *The Illusion of Caring: Children in Foster Care*. Boston: Beacon Press, 1973. (M)

Gil, David. *Violence Against Children*. Cambridge: Harvard University Press, 1970. (P)

Gil, David G. "What Schools Can Do About Child Abuse." *Childhood Education* 52, no. 2 (1975): 58-62. (M)

Groth, A. Nicholas. *Men Who Rape: The Psychology of the Offender*. New York: Plenum Press, 1979. (S)

Halperin, Michael. *Helping Maltreated Children: School and Community Involvement*. St. Louis: C. V. Mosby Co., 1979. (M)

Helfer, Ray E., and Kempe, C. Henry. *Child Abuse and Neglect: The Family and the Community*. Cambridge, Mass.: Ballinger, 1976 (M)

———— and ———— eds., *The Battered Child*. Chicago: University of Chicago Press, 1974. (P)

Herman, Judith. *Father-Daughter Incest*. Cambridge, Mass.: Harvard University Press, 1981. (S)

Holmes, Sally A.; Barnhart, C.; Cantoni, L.; and Reymer, E. "Working with the Parents in Child Abuse Cases." *Social Casework* 56, no. 2 (1975): 3-12. (P)

Hopkins, J. "The Nurse and the Abused Child." *Nursing Clinics of North America* 5 (1970): 594. (P)

Jirsa, James. *Child Abuse and Neglect: A Handbook*. Madison Metropolitan School District, 545 W. Dayton St., Madison, WI 53703. (M)

Kadushin, A. *Child Welfare Services*. New York: Macmillan, 1974. (M)

Katz, Sanford N. *When Parents Fail: The Law's Response to Family Breakdown*. Boston: Beacon Press, 1971. (M)

Kempe, C. Henry, and Helfer, Ray E. *Helping the Battered Child and His Family*. Philadelphia: J. B. Lippincott Co., 1972. (M)

Kempe, R., and Kempe, C. *Child Abuse*, Cambridge, Mass.: Harvard University Press, 1978. (M)

Martin, H. P., ed. *The Abused Child: A Multi-Disciplinary Approach to Developmental Issues*. Cambridge, Mass.: Ballinger, 1976. (P)

Mulford, Robert. *Emotional Neglect of Children*. Denver: American Humane Association (P. O. Box 1266). (N)

Murdock, G. G. "The Abused Child and the School System." *Public Health* 60 (1970): 105. (P)

National Center on Child Abuse and Neglect. *Child Abuse and Neglect, Audiovisual Materials*. Washington, D. C.: U.S. Department of Health, Education and Welfare, 1977 (M)

Newberger, Eli H., and Daniel, Jessica H. "Knowledge and Epidemiology of Child Abuse: A Critical Review of Concepts." *Pediatric Annals* (March 1976). (P)

Open the Door on Child Abuse and Neglect: Prevention and Reporting Kit. Ohio Department of Public Welfare, Children's Protective Services, 30 East Broad St., Columbus, Ohio 43215. (M)

Polansky, N. A.; Borgman, R. D.; and Desaix, C. *Roots of Futility*. San Francisco: Jossey-Bass, 1972. (N)

_____: Chalmers, M. A.; Buttenweiser, E.; and Williams, D. P. "Isolation of the Neglectful Family." *American Journal of Orthopsychiatry* 49 (1979): 149-52. (N)

_____: Holly, C.; and Polansky, N. F. *Profile of Neglect: A Survey of the State of Knowledge of Child Neglect*. Washington, D. C.: Department of Health, Education and Welfare, Community Services Administration, 1975. (N)

Red Horse, J. E., et al. "Family Behavior of Urban American Indians." *Social Casework* 59 (1978).

Rush, Florence. *The Best Kept Secret*. Englewood Cliffs, N. J.: Prentice-Hall, 1980. (S)

Schmitt, B. D. "What Teachers Need to Know About Child Abuse and Neglect." *Childhood Education* 52 (1975): 58-62. (M)

Schmitt, Barton D., ed. *The Child Protection Team Handbook, New York:* Garland S.T.P.M. Press, 1978. (M)

Sgroi, Suzanne M. "Molestation of Children: The Last Frontier in Child Abuse." *Children Today* 4 (1975): 18-21.

Sherman, E. A.; Neuman, R.; and Skyne A. W. *Children Adrift in Foster Care*. New York. Child Welfare League of America, 1973. (M)

Soeffing M. "Abused Children Are Exceptional Children." *Exceptional Children* 42 (1975): 126-33.

Werner, Emmy E. "Cross-Cultural Child Development." *Children Today* (March/April, 1979).

Pamphlets Published by U.S. Government Printing Office

American Indian Law: Relationship to Child Abuse and Neglect. 1981. 56 pp. HE 23.1210: In 2   S/N 017-092-0071-5

Child Abuse and Neglect: A Self-Instructional Text for Head Start Personnel. 1977. 135 pp. il. HE 23.1108:C 43   S/N 017-090-00035-6

Child Abuse and Neglect Among the Military: A Special Report from the National Center on Child Abuse and Neglect. 9 pp. HE 23.1210:M 59   S/N 017-092-0074-0

Child Abuse and Neglect Prevention and Treatment in Rural Communities: Two Approaches. 1978. 213 pp. il. HE 23.1210:C 73   S/N 017-090-0040-2

Child Abuse and Neglect, The Problem and Its Management: Volume 2, The Roles and Responsibilities of Professionals. 1976. HE 1.480:P 94/v.2 S/N 017-092-00017-1

Community Approach: The Child Protection Coordinating Committee. 1979. 82 pp. HE 23.1210/4:C 33 S/N 017-092-00040-5

Early Childhood Programs and the Prevention and Treatment of Child Abuse and Neglect: For Workers in Head Start, Family Day Care, Pre-school and Day Care Programs. 1979. 76 pp. HE 23.1210/4: Ea 7 S/N 017-092-00044-8

Educator's Role in the Prevention and Treatment of Child Abuse and Neglect. 1979. 74 pp. HE 23.1210/4:Ed 8 S/N 017-092-00043-0

How to Plan and Carry Out a Successful Public Awareness Program on Child Abuse and Neglect. Rev. 1980. 71 pp. HE 23.1210/4:AW 1 S/N 017-092-0067-7

Interdisciplinary Glossary on Child Abuse and Neglect: Legal, Medical, Social Work Terms. Rev. 1980. 45 pp. il. HE 23.1210:G 51/ 980 S/N 017-092-0062-6

Planning and Implementing Child Abuse and Neglect Service Programs: The Experience of Eleven Demonstration Projects. 1977. 16 pp. il. HE 1.480:969 S/N 017-092-0023-5

Profile of Neglect: A Survey of the State of Knowledge of Child Neglect. 1975. 57 pp. HE 17.702:N 31 S/N 017-065-00006-8

Sexual Abuse of Children: Selected Readings. 1980. 193 pp. il. HE 23.1210:Se 9/2 S/N 017-090-00057-7

Parenting Skills Workshops

Responsive Parenting by Saf Lerman
American Guidance Service Publishers' Building
Circle Pines, MN 55014-1796

1-800-328-2560 (in Minnesota)
1-612-786-4343 (call collect)

Prevention Projects

Bridgework Theater
113 1/2 East Lincoln, Suite 3
Goshen, IN 46526
Carol Plummer, Project Director

Judith Little
Rt. 2 - Box 330B
Mebane, NC 27302
919-563-1890
(for information regarding Trainer's
Manual which includes 5th grade
curriculum)

OR

Alamana Caswell
Area Mental Health and Mental Retardation Project
Child and Youth Services
1946 Martin Street
Burlington, NC 27215
(for information regarding Parents'
Booklet)

Illusion Theater
Hennepin Center for the Arts
528 Hennepin Avenue
Minneapolis, MN 55403
612-339-4944
Cordelia Kent, Director
Applied Theater

C. Henry Kempe National Center
for the Prevention and Treatment
of Child Abuse and Neglect
1205 Oneida Street
Denver, CO 80220
(for annotated list of audiovisual
library loan materials for educators and
school personnel, students, community
groups, child welfare professionals,
medical personnel, lay therapists)

Puppet Shows

What Should I Do? (S)
Elfin Productions
P.O. Box 422
Williamsburg, MA 01096

Video Puppet Productions (S)
Child Sexual Abuse Prevention Project
Franklin/Hampshire Community Mental Health Center
76 Pleasant Street
Northampton, MA 01060

Audiovisuals for Educators and Community Awareness

Child Abuse and the Law
Motion Picture Co., Inc. 1977
  27 min. film. Available from
Perennial Educ. Inc., 477 Roger Williams
P.O. Box 855 - Ravinia
Highland Park, IL 60035

Child Abuse: Cradle of Violence
Prod: Mitchell-Gebhardt Film Co.
  22 min. film. Available from
J. Gary Mitchell Film Co., Inc.
2000 Bridgeway
Sausalito, CA 94965

Child Abuse and Neglect: What the Educator Sees
  15 min. filmstrip and cassette. Available from
National Audio Visual Center, GSA Order Section
Washington, DC 20409

Children: A Case of Neglect
  56 min. film. Available from
Macmillan Films, Inc.
34 S. MacQueston Parkway
Mt. Vernon, NY 10550

Cipher in the Snow (Emotional abuse or neglect)
  23 min. film. Available from
Brigham Young University, Media Marketing
West Stadium
Provo, Utah 84602

Fragile, Handle With Care (looks at abuser)
Produced by KTAR-TV Productions
  26 min. film. Available from
High Court of Southern California
100 Border Avenue
Solan Beach, CA 92075

Incest: The Victim Nobody Believes
Produced by Mitch Gebhardt Film Co.
  21 min. film. Available from
J. Gary Mitchell Film Co., Inc.
2000 Bridgeway
Sausalito, CA 94965

Lift a Finger: The Administrator's Role in Combating Child Abuse and Neglect
  12 min. slide & cassette. Available from
Education Professionals Development Consortium
1750 Seamist
Houston, TX 77008

The Sexually Abused Child
Cavalcade Productions, 1978
  10 min. film. Available from
Motorola Teleprograms, Inc.
4825 N. Scott Street
Schiller Park, IL 60176

We Can Help. Unit 15, Specialized Training for Educators
  15 min. filmstrip & cassette
National Center on Child Abuse and Neglect
P.O. Box 1182
Washington, DC 20013

Whose Child Is This?
Shands (Alfred) Productions, Louisville, Ky.
  30 min. video cassette. Available from
Junior League of Louisville, Inc.
627 Main Street
Louisville, KY 40202

Books or Pamphlets to Use with Children

Adams C., and Fay, J. *No More Secrets*. San Luis Obispo, Calif.: Impact Publishing Co., 1981 (school age) (S)

Bassett, C. *My Very Own Special Body Book*. Reading, Calif.: Hawthorne Press, 1980. (school age) (S)

Dolan, Edward F. *Child Abuse*. New York: Franklin Watts, 1980. (high school) (M)

Fay, J. *He Told Me Not to Tell*. Renton Wash.: King County Rape Relief, 1979. (school age) (S)

_____. *Good Touch, Bad Touch.* Norristown, Penna.: Rape Crisis Center of Montgomery County (P.O. Box 1179, 501 Swede St., Norristown, PA 19401) (S)

Haskins, James. *The Child Abuse Help Book.* Reading, Mass.: Addison Wesley Publishing Co., 1982. (junior high & high school) (M)

Hyde, Margaret O. *Cry Softly! The Story of Child Abuse.* Philadelphia: Westminster Press, 1980. (high school) (M)

Marshall, James. *George and Martha.* Boston: Houghton Mifflin, 1972. (school age) (S)

Sanford, L. *Come Tell Me Right Away: A Positive Approach to Warning Children About Sexual Abuse.* Fayetteville, N.Y.: Ed.-U Press, 1982. (school age) (S)

Stowell, J., and Diltzel, M. *My Very Own Book About Me.* Spokane, Wash.: Spokane Rape Crisis Network, 1981. (Lutheran Social Services of Washington, 1226 N. Howard, Spokane, WA 99201) (Teacher's guide available) (young children) (S)

Sweet, P. E. *Something Happened to Me.* Racine, Wis.: Mother Courage Press, 1981. (5-10 years) (S)

Williams, J. *Red Flag, Green Flag People.* Fargo, N.D.: Rape and Crisis Center, 1980. (P.O. Box 1655, Fargo, ND 58107) (5-9 years) (S)

Training Programs to Use With Children

Personal Safety Curriculum. Prepared by Shirley Provost Brown, through The Child Sexual Abuse: Education and Prevention Project (Geri Crisci, Project Director). Franklin/Hampshire Community Mental Health Center, 76 Pleasant Street, Northhampton, MA 10160. (A unit to sensitize children in all grades toward prevention and protection from sexual assault.)

Seattle Rape Relief Developmental Disabilities. 1825 South Jackson, Suite 102, Seattle, WA 98114. (Special education curriculum on sexual abuse designed for handicapped children.)

Sexual Abuse Prevention Program. Illusion Theatre, 528 Hennepin Avenue, Minneapolis, MN 55403. (Provides theater productions to use with children to protect from sexual abuse.)

Women Against Rape. Child Assault Prevention Project. P.O. Box 02084, Columbus, Ohio 43202. (Provides a program for use in schools; also a brochure describing various sexual abuse workshops.)

Audiovisuals to Use with Children

Boys Beware (6-12 grades) (S)
Film. Available from
AIMS Instructional Media, Inc.
626 Justin Avenue
Glendale, CA 91201

Child Abuse: Don't Hide the Hurt (school age) (M)
Film. Available from
AIMS Instructional Media, Inc.
626 Justin Avenue
Glendale, CA 91201

For Pete's Sake, Tell! (school age) (S)
Speak Up, Say No! (school age) (S)
  Filmstrips. Available from
Krause House
P.O. Box 880
Oregon City, OR 97045

Negative Touch: Ways to Say No. (school age) (S)
  Film. Produced and distributed by
Child Abuse Series, Society for Visual Education
1345 Diversey Parkway
Chicago, IL 60614

No More Secrets (school age) (S)
  Film. Produced under grant from NCCAN
Distributed by ODN Productions
74 Varick Street
New York, NY 10013

Some Secrets Should Be Told (school age) (S)
Sometimes It's Okay to Tattle (school age) (S)
  Filmstrips. Produced by
Massachusetts Society for the Prevention of
Cruelty to Children
Distributed by
Family Information Systems
69 Clinton Road
Brookline, MA 02146

Who Do You Tell? (school age) (M)
  Film. Produced by J. Gary Mitchell Film Co.
Distributed by MII Teleprograms, Inc.
4825 North Scott Street, Suite 23
Schiller Park, IL 60176

THE REVIEW BOARD

ALABAMA: Vanessa Carter, Bessemer; Robert J. Evans, Troy; Gwen Floyd, Blontsville; R.E. Johnson, Florence; Robert Luhmann, Cullman; Thomas McKibben, Dothman; Evelyn Mims, Tuscaloosa; Kathy Norris, Montgomery; Alton Powell, Geneva; B.R. Warren, Florence; Joan Word, Abbeville; Sally J. York, Anniston.

ALASKA: Karen Hines, Ketchikan; Betsy B. McHugh, Juneau; Marcia Romick, College.

ARKANSAS: David Bell, Batesville; Edna Koehler, Little Rock; Linda McDaniel, Van Buren; Sarah Sullivant, Pine Bluff; Jeanne Whitesell, Little Rock.

ARIZONA: Jane B. Cole, Paradise Valley; Gi Crist, Mesa; Bessie High, Mesa.

CALIFORNIA: Donna Bartram, Upland; Susan Beak-McNeil, Fort Bragg; Joan Brader, Fremont; Charles Cobb, Riverside; Adrian Conlin, Los Banos; Janis Corn, San Diego; Nancy R. Corral, Sacramento; Emma Joanne Dale, Seal Beach; P.Elliott, Fullerton; Dana T. Elmore, San Jose; Richard N. Goss, Los Angeles; Richard S. Greene, Fresno; Bettye E. Grelling, San Dimas; Nathan Kravetz, San Bernardino; Gerald Larue, Jr., Culver City; Linda Leyva, Fort Bragg; M.McElroy, Rialto; Loretta Mayer, Los Angeles; Mildred Messinger, Berkeley; Mary Miller, Dinuba; M.Y. Nelson, Capitola; Susan November, San Dimas; Mike Pack, Fresno; Alexandra J. Prober, Altadena; Estelle Raderman, Castro Valley; Betty Smith, Mendocino; Maryann Spinella, Los Angeles; Anna Stump, Ridgecrest; Pamela Swales, Cupertino; Emmy Lou Swanson, Fountain Valley; Julie M. Thompson, Redding; Raymond Traynor, Twentynine Palms; Jean Vallas, Hermosa Beach; Neva Wacker, Central Valley; Sheila Widoe, Redding.

COLORADO: Sharon Alexander, Westminster; Carolyn Bruton, Granby; Dorothy McDonald, Sterling; Cay J. Spitzer, Colorado Springs.

CONNECTICUT: Noreen Barney, Brookfield Center; Glenna Clark, Darien; Patricia Endress, Sherman; Marjorie F. Grant, Columbia; Margaret L.Jusyk, Southport; Dolores Whelan, Morris; Deborah Worst, Simsbury; Robert A. Yawin, Plainville.

DELAWARE: B. Boyles, Wilmington; Linda Cooper, Dover.

DISTRICT OF COLUMBIA: Trudy Todd, Washington.

FLORIDA: Louise Boudreau, Orlando; Janet Cass, Destin; Kathy Kilpatrick, Quincy; Julia D. Lafferty, Jacksonville; Stanley M. Lucas, Gainesville; Gwynne Pealer, Ocala.

GEORGIA: Judith Bell, Adrian; Paulette Proctor Harris, Augusta; Cricket Kelley, Tifton; Leo J. Kelly, Valdosta; Mindy Long, Athens; Jerry Rogers, Athens; Elaine R. Weinstein, Atlanta; Mae Whatley, Athens.

HAWAII: Victoria Bannan, Honolulu; Florentina Smith, Kapaau; Peter George Vlachos, Honolulu.

IDAHO: Gladys Kosty, Post Falls; Marsha Nakamura, Nampa.

ILLINOIS: Audrey Bauer, Sterling; Wilhelmenia M. Cater, Highland Park; Pam Combs, Springfield; Elizabeth DaGue, Godfrey; Terry Gillespie, Park Forest; Nancy Goble, Mendota; Irvin Green, Cottage Hills; Beverly Gregor, Justice; Edna Harper, Norris City; Kenneth L. Holehouse, Park Forest; Marcy Mills, Mendota; LaVerne Pence, Edwardsville; Barbara Penick, Wilmette; June Shelly, Wood Dale; Larry S. Sterett, Biggsville; Louise Sterett, Hinsdale; Sue Widmar, Barrington.

INDIANA: Don S. Balka, Notre Dame; Katherine Brill, Michigan City; Colleen Browning, Lafayette; Angela Casso-Haines, Woodburn; Janet M. Deal, Hobart; June R. Gilstad, Kokomo; Patricia Gwaltney, Petersburg; Beth Ann Kroehler, Muncie; Mary Pauterbaugh, Elwood; Elizabeth Sisk, Indianapolis; Patricia Wittman, Hagerstown.

IOWA: Helen Anderson, Walker; Hazel Buhler, Sioux City; Shirley M. Crawford, Ankeny; Penny Davidson, Des Moines; Ruth Carol Egeland, Keokuk; Velma Held, Davenport; Mark Henderson, Oskaloosa; Linda Hood, Afton; Barbara James, Des Moines; Peggy Jetmund, Jesup; Ruth Kohrt, Rock Rapids; Marilyn Lilja, Janesville; Bonnie Mansfield, Malvern; Doris Mauer, Cedar Falls; Edna Rassler, Albert City; Lois F. Roets, New Sharon; Perry Ross, Mt. Pleasant; Joyce Runyon, Orange City; Hallie Russell-Reynolds, Norwalk; Maxine Schelp, Buckingham; Audrey Snyder, Humboldt; Lucy Stamper, Wever; Marian Tansey, Casey; Donna Thomas, Cedar Falls; Dawn Williams-Boyd, Iowa City; Norma Woods, Council Bluffs.

KANSAS: Elsie Brazelton, Axtell; Mari Pat Brooks, Horton; Phyllis Carlson, Newton; Carrie Curtis, Olathe; W.Merritt, Caldwell; Harry Peterson, Jr., Topeka; Florine Richey, Medicine Lodge; Denise Warren, Derby; Phillip Wilson, Fairway.

KENTUCKY: Nancy Demartra, Louisville; Margaret Hardesty-Day, Russellville; Mona Krone, Owenton; John Taylor, Murray.

LOUISIANA: Maggie Clemons, Lafayette; Billie Freisen, Lake Charles; LaFaye B. Graham, DeRidder; Sharon G. Luke, Mamou; Anne F. Perrett, Logansport; Mary G. Royston, Gray.

MAINE: Mary Cunningham-Hogan, Grove; Faith Garrold, Searsport; Alicia Harding, Cumberland.

MARYLAND: Ruby Clay, Fort Washington; Barbara Dewitt, Rockville; Judith Free, Baltimore; William J. Irwin, Laurel; Joyce Perry, Silver Spring; Margaret Petrella, Mt. Airy; Joan M. Reid, Chestertown; Claire Ritterhoff, Baltimore; Lynda Walker, Baltimore; Rosalind Yee, Camp Springs.

MASSACHUSETTS: Odetta Amarelo, Fall River; Thelma Barkin, Newton Center; Frances S. Baxter, Falmouth; Barbara Black, Holbrook; Ronald Brush, Sr., Burlington; Isabella C. Chang, Shrewsbury; William Day, Forestdale; Irene Duprey-Gutierrez, Lakeville; Cynthia E. Glass, Natick; Evelyn Hill, Auburn; Louise McLead Jordan, Needham; John Joyce, Burlington; Mary Kramer, Chelmsford; Kathleen MacDonald, Marshfield; Jerrold E. Rosen, Swampscott; Carrie Shultz, Centerville; Daniel T. Smith, Holyoke; MaryBeth S. Smuts, Norton; Judith Wilhelmy, Lowell.

MICHIGAN: Doris Anderson, Eagle; Janice Banka, Warren; Frances Baron, Zeeland; Betty Barry, Michigan Center; Edna Bates, Grand Blanc; Helen Blythe, Hudsonville; Peggy Cutler, Bloomfield Hills; Kathie D. Dugan, Comstock Park; Margaret Hamill, Muskegon; Marge Holland, Gould City; Rande Horn, DeWitt; Fran Kujda, Adrian; Sue Amspaugh Mellendorf, Otisville; Marlene Morlock, Clarkston; Kathy Overholser-Kalmer, Roseville; Patricia Ritner, Troy; Robert H. Rogers, Hartford; Carol Smallwood, Cheboygan; Marilyn Sprinkle, Olivet; Marion Trainor, Detroit; Albertina Weinlander, Big Rapids.

MINNESOTA: Bettie Arthur, Austin; Ronald Barron, Bloomington; Larry Barton, Bemidji; Leonard Bergquist, Moorhead; Pat Fillmore, Moorhead; Curtis J.Gilbertson, Byron; Sandra Gordon, Moorhead; Mary Keith Greene, Shafer; Jack Hartjes, St. Cloud; Charlotte Iiams, Moorhead; John Johansson, Detroit Lakes; Susan Mansfield, Winona; James Rowe, Marshall; Carol Sandbakken, Prior Lake; Debbi Wingert, Mound.

MISSOURI: Marvin Beckerman, St. Louis; Dee Boucher, Kansas City; Joseph Caliguri, Kansas City; Nancy Cramer, Kansas City; Rita K. Gram, St. Louis; Ruth Keeling, St. Louis; Margery Rich, Marshfield; Jeanne Schade, O'Fallon; Nancy Wandling, St. Louis; Betty Winder, Carthage.

MONTANA: Stephen L. Coffman, Billings; Jim and Joyce Litz, Missoula; Stanley Morse, Great Falls; Sharon Pereogy, Crow Agency; Jeane Rhodes, Whitefish.

NEBRASKA: Peggy Brendel, Omaha; Joyce E. Chapman, Bridgeport; Terry L. Erion, Cozad; Moira Fallon, Omaha; Harriett M. Johnson, Hastings; Carolyn J. Lane, Omaha; Joan Olsen, Hartington; Carolyn Pointer, Elmwood; Avonell Prochaska, Walthill.

NEVADA: Mike Morcom, Reno.

NEW JERSEY: Mary R. Bair, Dayton; Ronne Bassman, Englewood; Adele D. Bergen, Glen Rock; Ernest Brattstrom, Jr., Pitman; Anne M. Cancelmo, Pine Hill; Lawrence Cornell, Middlesex; Ruth E.Cullen, Township of Washington; Nina Davis, Bridgewater; Ann DeVenezia, Mountain Lake; Rita Fenichel, Livingston; Deborah S. Firkser, Elizabeth; Linda Fyne, Fords; Charlotte Gessler, Linden; Esther Gluskin, Ocean; Kathleen V. Haddon, Pennsauken; Sarah Heskins, Upper Saddle River; Peter S. Hlebowitsch, Princeton; Trisha Jones, Stanhope; J.Kapp, Jackson; Judith Kawalek, Bayonne; Doris Kneppel, Kinnelon; Mary Sue Koeppel, Pitman; Alex Paul Koharski, Neptune; Judith H. Kohlbach, Augusta; Charlotte Koslo, Hackettstown; R.M. leRiche, Passaic; Virginia Magnus, Medford; Anne Millard, Randolph Township; Frances B. Moldow, Fair Lawn; Louise H. Moore, Pennsville; Adele O. Oberlander, Cherry Hill; Marie Parry, Wall; Judith Foss Petry, Pompton Lakes; Ann Rice, Roselle Park; Leslie A. Rothman, North Bergen; Donna Rovento, Guttenberg; Joseph Sperlazza, Jersey City; Elaine Wallenburg, Haddonfield; William Winegardner, Gloucester; Myra Witmer, Freehold.

NEW HAMPSHIRE: Mary Carnie, Richmond; Lois E. Kenick, South Lyndeborough; Henry A.L. Parkhurst, Winchester; Nancy Sanborn, Enfield; Christine M. Sweeney, Keene.

NEW MEXICO: Paulette Buche, Estancia; Joyce Hodges, Hobbs; Edna McClung, Deming; Georgia Randolph, Los Alamos.

NEW YORK: Dianne Cicero, Mt. Morris; Marion Ellen Dexheimer, Howard Beach; Beth M. Teitelman, New York; Sally Walters, Canandaigua; John H. White, New York.

NORTH CAROLINA: Bonnie Blanton, Sherrills Ford; Marion Boyd, Charlotte; Debbie Cassels, Winston-Salem; Lorene H. Freeman, Hudson; Kathryn Herbert, Durham; Joan Lance, Asheville; Judith L. Nixon, Fayetteville; Sandra Phillips, Edenton; Frances M. Rash, Southmont; Mintie S. Saintsing, Thomasville; Charles Ward, Lenoir.

NORTH DAKOTA: Pat Fillmore, Fargo; Timothy L. Morris, Sherwood; Lillian Thorstad, Fargo; Bonnie Wilson, Bismarck.

OHIO: Jennifer Anspach, Covington; Linda Ater, Canton; R.Blosser, Findlay; Diane Boyer, Pataskala; Barbara Brim, Ada; Anne Engel, Westlake; Georgia Eshelman, Canton; Theresa Fox, Campbell; Ruth Hinebaugh, Clinton; Patricia Hurbean, Athens; J.Jackson, Lisbon; Victoria Kilbury, Dublin; Margaret Kirkland, Columbus; Karen Koehler, Hicksville; Lynne Lewicky, Cleveland; Peter Lymber, Youngstown; Peggy Treece Myles, Wauseon; Rita Pastor, Lakewood; Melinda Peters, Columbus; Mary Regas, Medina; Waneta M. Rodeheffer, Bowling Green; Joanne Schroeder, Wadsworth; Sylvia J. Seymour, Massillon; Virginia H. Stelk, Mount Vernon; Cynthia Thomas, Toronto; Christine W. West, Fairview Park; Janet Wojnaroski, Kent; Penelope H. Ziegler, Newark.

OKLAHOMA: Margaret Jane Couch, Tulsa; Joyce Grisham, Norman; Norma Marshall, Westville; Jeane Pearson, Durant; Claudia Swisher, Norman.

OREGON: Eileen Adee, Medford; Kathryn Blomquist, Beaverton; Cheryl Browne, Winston; Linda Deardorff, Reedsport; Gary Delvin, Lebanon; Carrol K. Harrison, Portland; Laura Henderson, Corvallis; Elaine Krause, Oregon City; Julie Thomas-Haskell, Beaverton; Joel S. Turvey, Beaverton; Ruth K. Warner, Portland; Cheryl E. Wesse, Winston.

PENNSYLVANIA: Yvonne Bair, Lancaster; Robert E. Baron, McKeesport; Vanessa Baugh, Harrison City; Rodney Boyer, Stowe; Carole Briggs, Brookville; Mary AnnCastelli, Chambersburg; D.Catley, Pittsburgh; Wilhelmina T. Decock, Kittanning; Eugenia Eden, East Stroudsburg; Richard Feil, Mansfield; Paula Fissel, Harrisburg; Gail Flinchbaugh, Seneca; Eleanore C. Hibbs, Perryopolis; Pearl Hoffman, Gettysburg; Joseph Homsher, West Chester; Madelin H. Knoll, Ambler; Mike Komlos, Ambridge; Evelyn Liebowitz, Elkins Park; Felicia Lincoln, Kennett Square; Norma McLean-Nish, Lansdale; Sheila Marcy, Aldan; Carla J.S. Messinger, Allentown; Ben A. Mule, California; Janet Olson, Pittsburgh; Dorothy C. Ott, Pittsburgh; Joann Patterson, Belle Vernon; B.J. Penrod, Johnstown; Eileen Pocius, Scranton; Pam Rader, Douglassville; Marsha Resinol, Pittsburgh; Erma Rohrer, Lebanon; Edith L.Rummel, Ligonier; Barbara Schleicher, Harrisburg; Mimi Schmitt, Bernville; Rita M. Schreinert, West Lawn; Ruth E. Sebastian, Harrisburg; Richard Shick, Mansfield; Myrna H. Slick, Holsopple; Celestine Sofilka, Pottsville; Elbert S. Solt, Lehighton; Santosh Vachher, Richboro; Marjorie B. Weest, Havertown; Melissa Yates, Perkasie; Kathleen D. Yothers, Wilkinsburg.

PUERTO RICO: Carmen Monge, Rio Piedras.

RHODE ISLAND: John Finnegan, Hopkinton; James Twining, Warwick.

SOUTH CAROLINA: Adell Adams, Columbia; Martha Barry, Hartsville; Richard Culyer, Hartsville; Beulah White, Georgetown; Bill D.Whitmire, North Myrtle Beach.

SOUTH DAKOTA: Nancy Lee Myers, Beresford; Avis Schafer, Florence; John W. Taylor, Brookings.

TENNESSEE: Cathy Bailey, Trezevant; Cheryl N. Fant, Memphis; Ruth A. Gadsden, Nashville; Margaret Gamble, Franklin; Frances Lovell, Kingsport; John W. Myers, Cookeville; Wanda Myers, Greeneville; Elizabeth Oakberg, Oak Ridge; Diann Poston, Rickman; Andrew M. Poston, Nashville; Elizabeth Ridenour, Knoxville; Louise S. Smith, Brentwood; Frances Sumner, Clarksville; Mary Thomas, Greeneville; Nancy Webb, Nashville.

TEXAS: Mary Margaret Clark, Eastland; Wendy Drezek, San Antonio; Lorraine Harrison, Odessa; Delores Hattox, Beaumont; Marcie Helmke, New Braunfels; Farrell F. Hogg, Abilene; Georgia Kelly, Lancaster; Hattie Kinder, Midway; Charles McGibbon, San Antonio; Molly Nunnelly, San Antonio; Ramona Pate, El Campo; Ella F. Proctor, Dallas; Linda Tanner, Houston.

UTAH: Joseph F. Bowman, Salt Lake City; J. Merrell Hansen, Provo; Grace Hiatt, Salt Lake City.

VERMONT: Sheila Mable, Springfield; Barbara La Pointe, Montpelier; John Willard, Vergennes.

VIRGINIA: J. Austin, Arlington; Phyllis L. Barton, Alexandria; Evelyn Beamer, Woodlawn; V.Lucy Boley, Lynchburg; Marjory Brown-Azarowicz, Fairfax; Linda Doggins, Yorktown; Deborah J. Dyer, Virginia Beach; Ellen Lee B. Elliott, Manassas; Jean Frey, Falls Church; Kathy Geiman, Stephens City; Youtha C. Hardman, Orange; Dorothy Harris, Clarksville; Cynthia L. McVay, Alexandria; Marilyn Maxson, Blacksburg; Beth Nelson, Radford; Pat Owen, Richmond; Lynne Schulz, Troy; Sallie Spiller, Roanoke; Joyce K. Tamer, Arlington; Yvonne V. Thayer, Radford; Pamela Walker, Alexandria.

WASHINGTON: Sheila Bell, Spokane; J. Wesley Crum, Ellensburg; Brooke L. Dillon, Auburn; Shirley Erwin, Snoqualmie; Mary L. Gleb, Burton; Ruth Glover, Tekoa; Nancy Hansen, Gig Harbor; Deanna H. Ray, Longview; Annamarie Lavieri, Bainbridge Island; Joyce Mateicka, Yakima; Fannie P. Ott, Ritzville; Guy-June Priest, Raymond; Sandra Smith, Quilcene; Pam Verner, Burlington; J.C. Welch, Outlook.

WEST VIRGINIA: Pat Bradley, Morgantown; Henrietta W. Keyser, Huntington; Margaret Phillips, Ridgeley; Debi Smith, Clay; Elizabeth Walter, Shepherdstown; Barbara Watts, St. Albans; Katherine H. Wilt, Harpers Ferry.

WISCONSIN: Pat Andress, Chippewa Falls; Robert Appelholm, Milltown; Gregory Bradley, Randolph; Evelyn Castellion, Wautoma; Linda Gail Davidson, Burlington; Doris Delzer, Kewaskum; Vivian R. Haefs, Wisconsin Rapids; Edith Johnson, Oshkosh; Carol Kloes, Three Lakes; Helen Lambron, Milwaukee; Catherine A. Meier, Milwaukee; Kathy Menaker, Waukesha; Lynda H. Moon, Beloit; Sharon Moser, Manitowoc; Sue Peterson, La Crosse; Peter Roop, Appleton; E.J. Scharrschmidt, Wausau; R.M. Schreiber, Waterloo; Nadine Day Sieber, Oshkosh; Marilyn Sjostrom, Athens; Wilmarth A. Thayer, Wittenberg; Judith Winzenz, Appleton.

WYOMING: H. Marie Boultinghouse, Moorcroft; Helen Fitch, Gillette; Ron Gray, Cheyenne.

FOREIGN: Richard C. Dye, APO NY.